AF429790

THE ISLAM WE MISS

THE ISLAM WE MISS

MOHAMMED MOHIUDDIN

CONTENTS

PREFACE

I have been fortunate to be born into a Muslim family, with parents who raised me with a traditional Sunni understanding. Throughout my life, Allah's guidance and mercy (*rahmah*), have brought me great professional, material, and family successes. This is not to say that the journey has been entirely easy, but nonetheless, as I look back on my life, I've come to recognize certain essential truths about Islam that might shed light on the condition of Muslims today.

While Islam remains a tremendous gift to mankind, today's Muslim does not reflect the greatness of the Prophet's (pbuh) companions. While materialism, dishonesty, and disunity have corrupted the minds of many Muslims, the constant barrage of Islamic books, videos, and lectures have failed to stem the spiritual and intellectual deterioration we are experiencing.

For the longest time I have struggled to find a reason why we are unable to truly connect to the religion of Allah. Why do we continue to pursue material distractions, while wrapping ourselves in a veneer of performative religiosity?

This book is my attempt to find what we have lost—an essential understanding of Islam that must have slipped away from us some point between the Prophet's time and our own. I have never been interested in the re-interpretation of a new Islam, but rather the re-discovery and re-invigoration of what has been buried just under our feet. If some of what I say might seem new, it is likely a testament to how far away we have moved from where we ought to be.

I sincerely hope that whatever ideas I can uncover in this book will be a source of discussion, insight, and guidance for my children and their children too--the very same insight that was given to Abraham, buried, and then rediscovered by our beloved Prophet Muhammad (pbuh)*. In what seems to be increasingly uncertain times, my deepest wish is that my family will not only understand Islam as I now do, but manifest its sweetness and purity at a time when the world will need it most. Ameen.

Mohammed Mohiuddin

October 7, 2020

* *I would recommend that this book not be read in a traditional manner from cover to cover but be read a chapter at a time as a family project and discussed adding personal experiences to foster deeper understanding of key issues that might have been missed and are necessary to build a real Islamic identity.*

INTRODUCTION

Born into an Indian Muslim family, I have practiced Islam for much of my early life in a very traditional way performing the standard rituals (five pillars) without a great deal of thought or introspection. After settling my family in America, it became increasingly essential to examine my place in a dominant culture that seemed to overwhelm the little knowledge and beliefs I had brought with me from home. I was fortunate to find support from the small community of about twelve Muslim families in my locality who helped anchor and preserve my Muslim identity, beliefs and practices. The community alone, however, was not enough to help me pass my traditions and beliefs on to my American children. Fortunately, this was also the time of a significant influx of Muslims from Asia, and I am sure the growing community was experiencing the same insecurity I was feeling about the survival of Islam in this country. As a result, many immigrant Muslims started to build organizations (ISNA, ICNA, etc.), which started a great awakening of Islam across the United States. This provided a tremendous source of fellowship and also a new way of looking at Islam in a more thoughtful manner where the emphasis began to shift from what we did (rituals) to why we did it.

I am indeed indebted to the many scholars who guided my journey of introspection. I am especially indebted to one scholar in particular, Imam Zakiuddin Sharfi, who settled in my community and made heroic efforts to educate our small circle of immigrant Muslims. While his fire and brimstone approach often turned some people away from his classes, it also began to engage many others who had long been on the sidelines.

Throughout our time together, I was fortunate to engage in countless intellectual debates with him in an effort to moderate some of his more extreme views. These discussions required me to first bring myself up to speed on various religious topics before I could engage him in meaningful discussions. Imam Zaki's insights and academic support helped me become a student of Islam as well as a more committed adherent.

I am not an Islamic scholar, but a practicing lay Muslim. As a physician-scientist, I have dedicated my adult life to education, caring for patients, clinical and biological research and publication, and of course raising a family. My career has taken me to various cities, each with their unique Muslim communities. Reflecting on these experiences, I have been able to reach some unfortunate conclusions.

First and foremost, I have recognized that many of us have diminished the practice of Islam to a transactional mindset. Khutbas preach that the intensity and quantity of our rituals are our key to heavenly rewards. This is especially so during masjid fundraising and disaster relief. Those who donate in this world, will be rewarded with a house in paradise. Those who attend salat regularly in the masjid will obtain the reward of Hajj in the Hereafter. Lost in this discussion is the possibility of doing something for the pleasure of Allah alone? There are many, many Muslims who volunteer and do good for the pleasure of Allah. In most communities this happens to be a small minority and they are the same people who rise to the occasion for every task. Meanwhile the majority of congregations are passive bystanders unless they are lining up for a free community dinner.

This universal passivity is most profoundly exhibited during the frequent duas for oppressed Muslims around the world. It is expected that because of the quantity of duas we make, Allah will take some action. Again we see the transactional element to this type of ritual. Certainly making dua for the oppressed is the least we can do, but the expectation that Allah will do something because we did something is a false assumption.

The Prophet's (pbuh) example makes it clear that while dua was essential, it was never enough. In every instance, action and sacrifice was required to change the direction of history and overcome the forces of evil. Yet in today's light, we see that while more masjids are being built and more Muslims are turning towards ritual Islam, the spirit of Islam remains weak. The image and achievement of Muslims as a community is falling further and further behind other nations and civilizations, and we have to ask why is this happening, specifically when Allah has clearly promised Muslims success in this world.

As a scientist, I look at our community status as a failing experiment. When a scientist conducts an experiment; he looks at three things. First he has a hypothesis. Then he develops a methodology to test the hypothesis. If both are correct, he has a successful result. However, if the results are not what was expected, repeating the experiment again and again, without making any change in the hypothesis or the methodology would be considered futile if not insane. We can look at the practice of religion in a similar fashion. A set of true beliefs, with the right practice should lead to ultimate success:

Belief + Practice = Success in this World & Hereafter
(*deen*)   (*amal*)

Belief in Allah as the Supreme Creator lies at the fundamental core of Islam. Our methodology is the way we follow the guidance of Allah as laid out for us in the Quran and Sunnah. Though we may think we are doing all the right things, success seems to elude, no matter how many times we repeat the same experiment. As a scientist, one has to conclude that either the hypothesis is wrong or the methodology must be preventing us from reaching the desired result. Because the hypothesis clearly cannot be wrong (as this is Allah's word), our methodology (practice of Islam) must be the problem. In the Quran Allah says:

"You are the best nation produced [as an example] for mankind. You enjoin what is right and forbid what is wrong and believe in Allah. If only the People of the Scripture had believed, it would have been better for them." *(Sure Al Imran 3:110)*

Historically we have seen what Muslim success looks like. We have seen the great and explosive expansion of Muslim influence during the early years of the Prophet (pbuh) and the empires that followed. We have seen the dynamism of Muslim scholars and thinkers, many of whom have laid the foundational understanding of modern civilization. The world marveled at the Muslim world and came to learn from us and copy our humanity and our culture. When and how did we lose the zenith of human achievement to becoming the pariahs of this world?

History has seen many great civilizations, but what sets the Islamic civilization apart from others was the egalitarian nature of its core belief. I would argue that our decline can be tied to a return to a pre-Islamic (jahilliya) pyramid hierarchy. The infusion of an elitist mentality resulted in a free for all, where Muslims stopped being the keepers of their brothers and self-promotion at the expense of others became rampant. We saw this play out among Muslim state entities, who were unable to mount a unified resistance to colonial domination. Muslims fell back on prayer as their salvation instead of reconstituting the Umma into a collective strength. Meanwhile recognizing that Islam will always be a great potential force, Europeans have endeavored over the last several centuries to weaken one of its fundamental strengths (the community) by sidelining religion to a solely private affair, all the while promoting individual exceptionalism as the only true achievement. "Separation of church and state," has brainwashed Muslims into redefining piety as the practice of private rituals rather than public service and the constant struggle to promote community welfare.

Reclaiming the true essence of Islam is easier said than done for it requires a wholesale reorienting of cultural and religious norms that have redefined Islam and what it really means to be a complete Muslim. We must stop thinking of Islam as a religion of peace and more as a religion of struggle to live up to Allah's description of us as the "best nation for mankind." It means we have to be the leaders and not followers. It calls for a breakdown of traditional thinking and education regarding many areas of Islamic thought.

Although I have written my thoughts over a long period of time, I have found that understanding Islam is very much an evolutionary process. Though I may have felt that I knew much about Islam, early in my adult life, I only truly started to understand the scope and depth of Islam when I began to ask the question "WHY?" Why are the rituals of Islam important? Why is Allah testing us? Why are Muslims failing? Unfortunately, I have found many scholarly answers largely unsatisfactory.

In the next several chapters I have endeavored to put some of my thoughts to paper. I am not a scholar, but I am a scientist. While a scholar-class education can be of tremendous value, it also carries the danger of engendering subconscious biases which further defend failing educational/institutional systems. I pray for Allah's forgiveness if my conclusions exceed my expertise, but to be clear, my intention is to start a conversation rather than give an ultimate prescription.

1 | THE PURPOSE OF LIFE

It is vital to understand mans' relationship to his Creator and what He desires from us in this life on Earth.

Why are we here? Why were we created and for what purpose? These are age-old questions that many philosophers have attempted to answer. Ironically, the very clearest explanation has received the least attention.

Professor Jeffry Lang, a seasoned mathematician, who went from being a Christian, to rejecting God altogether, to embracing Islam, discovered the purpose of life in the first few pages of the Quran. If we turn to the second surah, Al Baqarah, we encounter the story of Adam (pbuh), the first human to be created by Allah.

For Dr. Lang, here was the clearest explanation of the purpose of life (see Professor Lang's books and YouTube presentations especially at Ames, Iowa 2011). It is unfortunate that so few people, especially Muslims are aware of Professor Lang's insights. Few thousands of people have watched his explanations, while millions watch programs on obscure religious subjects that focus on far less relevant minutiae.

Allah says multiple times in the Quran:

"And We created not the heavens and the earth, and all that is between them, in play." *(Surah Al Dukhan 44:38, Surah Anbiya 21:16, Surah Sad 38:27, Surah Mu'minun 23:115)*

Should we not take this statement seriously and try to understand the reason why Allah is repeatedly asserting that there is a very specific purpose in the creation of the Heavens and the Earth and all that is in between? We are told that there is a very specific purpose for our creation and it is for us to discern that purpose from what Allah has revealed to us directly through His revelations and the use of the faculties He has endowed us with.

The very first question to be answered is what kind of creation is "man." Allah has said that man was created from dust (or black mud) (Surah Al An'am 6:2) and into this Allah breathed some part of His spirit (Surah As-Sajjdah 32:9). The first man to be created as such was Adam and from him was created Eve. Allah then taught Adam the names of many things. This implies that Allah created a uniquely intelligent being with the capacity to "learn." He also said that He planned to place him on Earth as His vice-regent with authority over His other earthly creatures. The verses of Surah Baqarah (2:29-39) lay out the process of Adam's creation, his growth, his status among creation, and the subsequent planned role Allah had assigned to him:

"It is He who created for you all of that which is on the earth. Then He directed Himself to the heaven, [His being above all creation], and made them seven heavens, and He is Knowing of all things.

And [mention, O Muhammad], when your Lord said to the angels, "Indeed, I will make upon the earth a successive authority.

They said, "Will You place upon it one who causes corruption therein and sheds blood, while we declare Your praise and sanctify You?" Allah said, "Indeed, I know that which you do not know."

And He taught Adam the names of all things; then He placed them before the angels, and said:" Tell me the names of these things if you are right."

They said, "Exalted are You; we have no knowledge except what You have taught us. Indeed, it is You who is the Knowing, the Wise."

He said, "O Adam, inform them of their names." And when he had informed them of their names, He said, "Did I not tell you that I know the unseen [aspects] of the heavens and the earth? And I know what you reveal and what you have concealed."

And [mention] when We said to the angels, "Prostrate before Adam"; so they prostrated, except for Iblees. He refused and was arrogant and became of the disbelievers.

We said: "O Adam! Dwell you and your wife in the Garden; and eat of the bountiful things therein as you will; but approach not this tree or you run into harm and transgression."

But Satan caused them to slip out of it and removed them from that [condition] in which they had been. And We said, "Go down, [all of you], as enemies to one another, and you will have upon the earth a place of settlement and provision for a time."

Then Adam received from his Lord [some] words, and He accepted his repentance. Indeed, it is He who is the Accepting of repentance, the Merciful.

We said, "Go down from it, all of you. And when guidance comes to you from Me, whoever follows My guidance – there will be no fear concerning them, nor will they grieve.

And those who disbelieve and deny Our signs – those will be companions of the Fire; they will abide therein eternally."

This story is in sharp contrast to Christian and Jewish traditions, where God is surprised and angered by Adam's betrayal and punishes him by casting him away on Earth. What kind of God would not have known what Adam's actions were going to be? Why would he be surprised or angered? Was he just looking for an excuse to punish Adam? The most important narrative of man's creation makes no sense in their tradition. In contrast, the Quran lays out a clear plan by an All-Knowing God who has a reason for every action. After all, does not Allah say, "We created not the Heavens and the Earth and all that is between them for play"? (44:38)

Why did Allah ask Adam not to go near that tree? Here we see that Adam is given an opportunity to exercise choice. Adam was created with a free will unlike most any other of Allah's creation and an ability to make independent decisions. When Adam ate the fruit of the tree Allah had prohibited, Adam had made his first choice and exercised his independent will.

As per Allah's plan, Adam was now ready to move to the next stage of his growth. Allah shows Adam the scope of His Mercy in forgiving his transgression and accepting his repentance. Allah then places Adam on Earth with the charge of being His "vice-regent" (caretaker) over all the dominion of the Earth. Allah promises to send him guidance from time to time to foster his growth and He reassures all those who pay attention to this guidance, that they will "have nothing to fear nor will they grieve." (2:274)

Man, as with Adam, will have free choice to accept or reject this guidance. Allah repeatedly emphasizes in the Quran, "there is no compulsion in religion. The right course has become clear from the wrong" (Surah Al Baqarah, 2:256) and it is for individuals to make their choice. The Quran also makes clear how man is to make his choice. This choice not only comes through following explicit revelation, but also though man's unique capacity for intellect and reason. As explained by Dr. Lang, Allah says in different verses that the choice is clear for those who use their knowledge (8 times) and reason (10 times) and those that have insight (16 times). The Quran also points out that those who reject His revelations are in manifest error (28 times) because instead of using their intellect they are foolish (3 times), ignorant (15 times) or only follow surmise and conjecture (9 times). Some blindly adhere to misleading traditions and cultural norms in spite of clear evidence of proof (7 times) to the contrary.

The Quran encourages man to think by repeatedly providing proofs and then asking questions such as "what do you think" (18 times) or "do you suppose" (7 times) or "have you considered" (13 times). Most telling of all, the Quran asks of those who reject His guidance, "do you even think" (18 times).

Why is the Quran asking these questions? Clearly the Quran wants men to make an independent choice of who and what they want to be. **This "choice" that man has been given is a fundamental reason for man to be placed on Earth.** Allah created man for a purpose and while he was in Heaven, Allah taught many things and also showed him the power of exercising his independent will in making choices. Allah shows man how to correct for his mistakes by asking for forgiveness and shows him His infinite Mercy. In all of this Allah is orchestrating human development. Man started off almost like a rough diamond that first has to be cut, then shaped and finally polished to produce the pristine polished jewel. Adam's time in Heaven was the period of his creation and the first cuts of the rough diamond. His life on Earth will see the shaping and the polishing of his personality. Those jewels that sparkle and shine will receive Allah's favor in the next life and those that incorporate imperfections will be discarded on the garbage pile.

"Whoever does righteousness, whether male or female, while he is a believer – We will surely cause him to live a good life, and We will surely give them their reward [in the Hereafter] according to the best of what they used to do." (Surah An-Nahal 16:97)

What and how is this shaping and polishing achieved? Allah makes this abundantly clear in the Quran that the life of this Earth is for man to grow in righteousness and good deeds. The Quran defines what traits man needs to acquire. First is to get to know Allah, his Lord and Creator through the words of His prophets.

"Allah is the one who created you, then provided for you, then will cause you to die, and then will give you life. Are there any of your "partners" who does anything of that? Exalted is He and high above what they associate with Him." (Surah Ar-Rum 30:40)

Almost in every chapter of the Quran Allah makes Himself known to mankind:

"Say, 'He is God, the One. God, the Absolute. He begets not, nor was He begotten. And there is none comparable to Him.'"
(Surah Ikhlas 112)

But Allah also asks man to acquire knowledge of the world and through the many brilliant signs of His Creation use his intellect to experience Allah's Magnificence. To seek knowledge is mentioned over eight hundred times in the Quran because in the application of this knowledge are lessons to fully understand the Creator and make a will-ful choice to establish his relationship and belief in the Almighty.

"Roam the Earth and observe how creation was initiated. (Surah Al Ankabut 29:20)

And say, "[All] praise is [due] to Allah. He will show you His signs, and you will recognize them. And your Lord is not unaware of what you do." (Surah An-Naml 27:93)

It is only with knowledge that man can fully accept the guidance that Allah has provided through the prophets and the Quran. Only when this certainty of belief enters his heart can man start to take his responsibility and duty to Allah seriously. Only then can he start the process of developing a Quranic personality:

"Whoever does righteousness, whether male or female, while he is a believer – We will surely cause him to live a good life, and We will surely give them their reward [in the Hereafter] according to the best of what they used to do." (Surah An-Nahal 16:97)

The word "righteousness" encompasses many attributes mentioned in the Quran. Righteousness is to believe in Allah, in the Last Day, the angel the books and the prophets.

"Righteousness is not that you turn your faces toward the east or the west, but [true] righteousness is [in] one who believes in God, the Last Day, the angels, the Book, and the prophets and gives wealth, in spite of love for it, to relatives, orphans, the needy, the traveler, those who ask [for help], and for freeing slaves; [and who] establishes prayer and gives zakah (obligatory charity); [those who] fulfill their promise when they promise; and [those who] are patient

in poverty and ailment and during battle. Those are the ones who have been true, and it is those who are the righteous."
(Surah Al Baqarah 2:177)

Righteousness is also to do good deeds (19:96). Righteousness is to be a man of character and develop traits of mercy, truthfulness, kindness, love for fellow man, caring, humility, justice, forgiveness, patience, gratitude and many more. Each of these traits mirrors the ninety-nine traits of Allah. Human traits, however, are limited by human intelligence, while Allah's traits are without limits. These traits, then become the ninety-nine facets of the diamond Allah has put on Earth. This is not an instant occurrence or an easy task. As the Quran states, it takes years to attain this maturity:

"When he attains full strength and reaches forty years, he says: "My Lord! Grant me the power and ability that I may be grateful for Your Favor which You have bestowed upon me and upon my parents." (Surah Al Ahqaf 46:15).

This process is therefore, one of development just like a fruit on a tree that starts as seed and turns into a flower. The flower then transforms into an unripe fruit that gathers nutrition and water from the plant and stays attached to the tree to ripen to a perfect specimen. However, during this process the fruit is challenged by wind and rain, by birds and worms, by disease and destruction. Those that make the journey successfully become the pride of the table, whereas those that fall of the tree are discarded to the garbage pile.

Similarly, during the process of man's maturation he is constantly challenged by a multitude of good and bad times. In fact Allah makes plain that these challenges are necessary and may be quite severe.

"And We will surely test you with something of fear and hunger and a loss of wealth and lives and fruits, but give good tidings to the patient,

Who, when disaster strikes them, say, "Indeed we belong to Allah, and indeed to Him we will return."

Those are the ones upon whom are blessings from their Lord and mercy. And it is those who are the [rightly] guided."
(Surah Al Baqarah 2:155-157)

Those who meet these challenges with conviction in Allah's promise are the ones who are successful like the sweetest of fruit on the tree. Deprivation and suffering are necessary as grit is to polish. How else can we create the sparkle and luster on the many faces of a diamond? If there is no suffering how can we learn compassion? If there is no hunger how can we learn empathy? If there is no disease how can we learn caring and if there was no death, would our hearts be made of stone?

"Seek Allah's help with patient perseverance and prayer. It is indeed hard except for those who are humble." (Surah Al Baqarah 2:45)

For those that achieve success in this trial of life on Earth, Allah has promised a tremendous reward in the Hereafter. They will reside therein with peace and comfort and will not want for anything.

"Indeed, Allah has purchased from the believers their lives and their properties [in exchange] for that they will have Paradise. They fight in the cause of Allah, so they kill and are killed. [It is] a true promise [binding] upon Him in the Torah and the Gospel and the

Quran. And who is truer to his covenant than Allah? So rejoice in your transaction which you have contracted. And it is that which is the great attainment." (Surah Tauba, 9: 111)

While Heaven is a beautiful reward and a goal to strive for, it is still a human goal and begs the question of whether this is all that Allah planned. Heaven cannot be just a super luxury retirement community. While it is not for us to question or know beyond what our prophets have relayed to us, Allah did create us as intelligent beings. If all Allah had wanted was to populate Heaven with human angels, He would just have to say, "Be!" and it would have happened instantly. After all, Allah does not need us. He also tells us that He, "did not create the Heavens and the Earth for play." Therefore, Allah must have a specific purpose and plan for those who chose the arduous path of polishing themselves when the rest of humanity chose the road of ease and indulgence.

While He has not revealed to us how He wishes to use these "gems," it is enough for us to consider that He has chosen this process as a means to His plan. Those who reject Allah will be discarded. Therefore, the example before us is like taking a college exam. While a pass is good enough, we have to work harder and single mindedly to be at the top of the list if we want to get to medical school. Similarly, while getting to jannah in the Hereafter may be good enough, being at the top of the list of people that Allah will call on for whatever his plan is, should be our goal. Though the competition may be fierce, it certainly must be something worth striving for.

Life is an opportunity full of meaning and promise. While others grab with their hands, we must seize it with our hearts and our minds. The former is the path of this world, the latter is the path to Allah.

Understanding the purpose of life to its logical conclusion also gives us the best opportunity to build a secure loving relationship with Allah. Allah taught Adam the names of all things and put man on Earth to perfect his character. Going back to the example of medical school, any student with a reasonable memory can memorize all the infor-mation. But what good is the minutiae without any practical under-standing? Likewise, once Adam was taught the names of all things, he was established on Earth to develop a workable understanding of that knowledge through inquiry and experience. As children of Adam, we too are asked to perfect character by understanding the knowledge given to us.

When prospective medical students are asked by admissions panels why they want to be a doctor, the most common response is, "I want to serve humanity." But only those who genuinely believe this are able to develop a lifelong passion for their work and derive long-term fulfillment in their careers. Similarly, those who want to get to the next world, are motivated by a genuine desire to be near Allah. Like medical school, this life is simply a preparatory stage. Now compare this to the transactional approach of many Muslims who are far more concerned with getting into heaven or staying out of hell. In the end, who will likely be more successful? Whose life can be better than the one who sincerely loves Allah and is constantly yearning to be near Him? In the words of Rabi'a al Basri, one of the great Sufi mystics:

"O Lord, if I worship You because of Fear of Hell,
then burn me in Hell;

If I worship You because I desire Paradise,
then exclude me from Paradise;

But if I worship You for Yourself alone,
then deny me not your Eternal Beauty."

2 | WHAT IT MEANS TO BE A MUSLIM

To be the best human being in the service of Allah.

When I look at the present Islamic civilization from a dispassionate scientific lens I find that the current state of the Muslim ummah is not a result of their weak faith or their lack of commitment to Allah and the Prophet (pbuh) but due to a fundamental lack of understanding of what Islam is all about. I believe we have lost ground in our understanding of religion by **our choice of words and how we express ideas**. We are too wedded to traditional words and ideas that were expressed a thousand years ago and had real meaning for the civilization of those times. While the language of the Quran remains eternal, the understanding of the singular significance of many words changes as civilizations evolve and the contextual application of language changes. Therefore, we do not need to reinvent Islam, but revitalize the understanding of what it really means to be a Muslim.

We can all agree that the Muslim community is in crisis. In spite of reaching almost a third of the global population, Muslim populations are under siege worldwide. Certainly there are more Muslims performing the religious obligations of Salat and Sawm and more Muslims at Umra and Hajj every year. And yet this quantitative increase in ritual has not borne the expected results. In our seemingly helpless state, generations of Muslim youth are getting disconnected from their Islamic roots. Perhaps they see a one-dimensional veneer of Muslim practice that is disconnected from the reality of personal existence. Why is there this disconnect? This is the real challenge for the Islamic community: to make the connection between theory and practice, and exemplify a living religion that others will whole heartedly embrace.

Many scholars repeatedly expound the thesis that we are disconnected from our Islamic roots and a more rigid adherence to practices of old will bring back the glory of Islam, not to mention the exuberance and joy of being Muslim. However, in spite of thousands of books, lectures, discourses and exhortations, there is a singular lack of movement in the mindset of the Muslim ummah. Rather, there seems to be a fatalistic view that Allah will make it all right in the end so long as we keep to the prescribed rituals. I believe that this approach is not a solution but an abdication of our responsibilities of what it really means to be a Muslim.

In an informal survey I have asked many family members, friends and even a few well-recognized scholars, all excellent Muslims, the simple question "what does it means to be a Muslim?" Surprisingly, the answers were all over the place. Some felt that anyone who takes the shahadah is a Muslim, while others felt that fulfilling the five pillars is necessary to be a Muslim. The scholars felt the answer to this question requires a whole lecture. While all of these answers were not wrong, they are answers to the question of "who is a Muslim?" not "what is a Muslim?" It is like the parable of the four blind men who touch different parts of the elephant and come to different conclusions; each more convinced than the other that they are correct. It is no wonder that with such an amorphous understanding of this most fundamental question we are not more lost than we are, walking around in the dark unable to see the light of the Quran.

The most intriguing answer of course is from the scholars of Islam. Why does it take a whole lecture to answer a simple question? They say that the simple answer to "what is a Muslim?" is, "one who submits to the Will of Allah." But to understand the "will" of Allah you have to understand everything that is in the Quran and Sunnah. While this may be true, it also institutionalizes the superiority of the scholar over the layperson, who cannot possibly know the extent of all that is in the Quran or even understand it. I see this as an example of a rocket built to fly man to the moon. A layperson understands this in simple terms as a transport to the moon. A scholar says that this is a "flying machine" and to understand what it does, you have to understand each nut and bolt of the machine. Then only can you understand its full function. It is no wonder that the vast majority of Muslims are sentenced to a life of ritual and why so many young Muslims are running from Islam.

Is there a simpler answer that will provide clarity and focus to the Muslim mind? I believe there must be a simpler approach. If we look at the companions of the Prophet (pbuh), few of them knew the entire Quran (much of it had not yet been revealed fully until much later) yet many of them were the best of Muslims. What was the secret that the Prophet (pbuh) used to transform a tribal, uneducated civilization into the best community imaginable? I believe it was the clarity and simplicity of the Prophet's message, coupled with a practical approach to attaining this vision.

The Prophet (pbuh) defined the vision and mission for Muslims in very simple terms. He instructed us to "submit to the Will of Allah," which he relayed in the Quran. If this one statement is broken down into its constituent parts, it can be interpreted as a vision component (future) "to achieve the Grace of Allah," and the mission component (present) "how to live a life." The Prophet (pbuh) then transformed a whole nation of "jahilliya" by establishing the mission for each and every Muslim who believed in this vision. Without this clarity of vision we do not have a mission and without the clarity of mission we cannot achieve our destination (vision).

When you ask most people what is Islam, they usually respond by saying "submission to the Will of Allah." If you ask them who is a Muslim, they respond by "one who submits to the Will of Allah." Unfortunately this is such an amorphous, passive statement, that it leaves non-Muslims feeling bewildered, and Muslim youth feeling disinterested. Our mistake is that we have rolled the vision and mission statements into one. The vision statement defines the ultimate goal. The mission statement is the action plan on how to achieve the ultimate goal.

This confusion stems not only from a lack of clear understanding, but also from the connotations of the word "submit." At the time of the Prophet (pbuh) the word "submit" was understood in a cultural context where the concept of authority was essential to individual and clan survival. But in today's world, wives do not submit to husbands, children do not submit to parents and men do not submit to authority except when it provides material well-being. The word "submit" is now disconnected from any concept of modern daily life especially for Muslim youth. In today's context, submission confers a wholly negative connotation. This is incredibly unfortunate, because the prophets were all sent to unleash human potential.

In today's world defining Islam solely as "Submission to the Will of Allah" has led many scholars to interpret Islam into narrow areas of rules and regulations that govern our life. In the Quran there are an extensive number of do's and dont's. In addition, the traditions of the Prophet (pbuh) have further defined the permissible (halal) and prohibited (haram). Many of these range from the very minute aspects of individual life to larger issues of community and conduct in war. These rules and regulations and their interpretations have now formed the codification of modern Islam's sectarianism rather than the representation of Allah's Will.

As the era of Islamic empires has passed, more and more of our religious scholars have blamed the decline of the Islamic civilization on the shortcomings of Muslims in "submitting to Allah." Every sermon (khutba) from the pulpit is about our failings to live by the "rules of submission." The Taliban came to power in Afghanistan to enforce these rules. They are not the only ones. In every community, large and small, in every masjid, urban or rural, there is a conflict between those who would impose a rigid definition that require mindless submission in religion (the so called fundamentalists) and the reactionary non-fundamentalists who promote a watered-down secular Islam.

Unfortunately, the word "fundamentalist" carries a negative connotation even though it should simply imply adherence to basic concepts of religion. Instead the term "submission" has come to describe a political tool used by the ruling class to control people's lives. The word "SUBMIT" is shouted out in the loudest voice from the pulpit, but the words "Allah's Will" is mentioned in a whisper hoping the Muslim will submit to the imams and pseudo-scholars who decry western and secular knowledge.

Jesus rebelled against the keepers of the temple because they controlled people's minds through submission to the high priest. Instead of liberating people, religion became an instrument of oppression. Jesus said, "The Sabbath was created for mankind, not man for the Sabbath." So it is today that religion is given to mankind to liberate him and make him a better person. Religion was not prescribed to be used as a sword by the rich or the powerful or for political gain.

Unfortunately defining Islam as "submission" has become part of the folklore of Islam. The dictionary defines "submission" as "to yield to governance or authority." When other men in the name of religion usurp this authority, it creates a slippery slope that violates the first dictum of the shahadah, "there is no God but the one God." The constant drum beat of "submission" also has a profound effect on the human mind, facilitating the subjugation of your God given intelligence to the will of other humans, especially reflected by the treatment of women in "Islamic communities." This loss of the human spirit is contrary to the liberation Islam came to bring. It has resulted in building cages in which the Muslim mind has been incarcerated for the last several centuries.

So how do we redefine the word "submit" so that it gives meaning and clarity to the truest purpose of Islam? I believe that the mission statement for Muslims should be redefined as: **"to be the best possible human being in the service of Allah."** The Quran has used the word

"Abd" (servant) to define who we are as a people. It is as a servant of Allah that we will attain his Mercy (vision). The Quran repeatedly used the word "righteous" (salaheen) in 31 verses to define those who Allah considers to be His servants. Righteousness therefore is the operational word for a Muslim's mission. To be truly righteous we have to become "the best possible human being in the service of Allah."

This mission statement "to be the best possible human being in the service of Allah" distills the whole essence of what it means to be a Muslim. Allah has appointed us as His viceroy on Earth (6:165) and tasked us to represent Him as embodied in His ninety-nine attributes. Our challenge is to represent him to the best of our human abilities in embodying these attributes. Therefore, to be the best possible human being in the service of Allah, we have to strive for excellence in our love for Allah and the Prophet (pbuh). We have to strive for excellence in knowledge of the Quran and Sunnah. We have to strive for excellence in our worship. We have to strive for excellence in our relationships with our family. We have to strive for excellence in acquisition of knowledge about the world around us. We have to strive for excellence in support of our community. We have to strive for excellence in our professions. We have to strive for excellence in our service to our fellow men. And we have to strive for excellence in protecting all of nature around us. Then and then only can we say that we are discharging our responsibility according to the Will of Allah and claim to be "the best community raised up for mankind" (Surah Al Imran 3:110).

Imagine the impact on young minds if they grow up with the mindset that they are required to be the best in each and every one of these endeavors. It is easy to understand and everyone can relate it to all aspects of their lives. This also creates an active purposeful framework for life. Imagine the impact when children from the earliest awakening of consciousness hear repeatedly their defining purpose in life. There is no longer an identity crisis of who they are and how they fit into their world. Imagine also the impact of telling a non-Muslim about your clear vision and mission of what is a Muslim in these terms as compared to the traditional lines of explanation. Most times non-Muslims, when they hear the traditional explanation, look at you cross-eyed and start theological discussions. However, no one can argue with the statement "a Muslim is one who strives to be the best human being possible." If every Muslim grows up with this identity and understanding, there is no limit to future possibilities because Allah has promised the kind of help that guarantees incredible success as exemplified by the achievements of the early Islamic civilizations.

Allah has said that Muslims are "the best people created for mankind" (Surah Al Imran 6:110). We just have to believe and live up to it by making this an essential part of our being.

3 | PROPHET MUHAMMAD (PBUH)

"La illaha illallah, Muhammad-ur-Rasullulah."

This creed is the central basis of the religion of Islam. After affirming that there is no God but the one God-Allah, Prophet Muhammad (pbuh) occupies the most venerated position in Islam. Allah has said that no one can get to know or love Allah unless he gets to know and love the Prophet (pbuh). One can get to know "about" the Prophet (pbuh) by reading books on his life and from listening to lectures by scholars. There is however a vast gulf between "knowing about him" and "getting to know" him. The difference is between reading a biography, and owning that knowledge such that it becomes part of one's own personality. Only when Prophet Muhammad's (pbuh) personality comes alive within you, can you say that you truly love him.

In history there have been many individuals who people follow with great emotional attachment. In the vast majority of cases they result from the tragic circumstances of their untimely deaths. Jesus (pbuh) and Hadrat Imam Hussein are two classic examples. Generation after generation of storytellers and poets have created great passion plays of their suffering. What follows is an emotional outpouring of attachment and love. But is this really love, or is this just love for the melodrama? What remains of the actual teachings of Jesus? It is certainly not the religion Jesus professed and practiced. Nonetheless, Christians love the stories of Jesus in the manger and Jesus bloodied and tortured with a crown of thorns being dragged to his death. So it is with Hadrat Imam Hussein. People lash themselves till they are bloodied as a sign of reverence. Yet while the world considers these examples as an exhibition of profound love, I find an inherent misunderstanding of the word "love."

The English language is pretty sterile when it comes to differentiating between different kinds of "love." Is the love of chocolates, the love of a vacation, and the love of a spouse the same? Unlike other languages that often have ten or more words to express different types of love, there are few useable words in English. Most people fail to distinguish the difference between the words "love" and "like." You can like many things in life, but "love" denotes some emotional connection. The indiscriminate use of the word "love" has reduced its significance from something special to things that are transient and temporary. Genuine "love" requires a commitment of your heart and soul. True love can be seen in the love of a mother for her child. Allah compares His love for humanity as seventy times greater than maternal love. At the same time Allah also asks us to love the Prophet (pbuh) more than we love our children. The question for us today is how much real love do we have for the Prophet? Do we even know him well enough to fall in love with him?

We know from the many books of Seerah that he was a descendent of Abraham (pbuh) through Abraham's son Ishmael (pbuh). He was born an orphan in Mecca in the tribe of Hashim in 570 C.E. (his father died six months before his birth). He was sent off to be wet nursed by a poor Bedouin woman in the desert as was the custom of the day, and he returned to his mother Amina several years later. Amina took him on a trip to visit relatives in Yathrib. On the return journey to Mecca, his mother fell ill and died at a wayside village called Abwa. At the age of six this poor child was now doubly orphaned. Imagine him witnessing the burial of his mother with tears streaming down his face!

Who was there to wipe those tears? Who was there to hold his hand? Who was there to calm his troubled heart? How is it that our focus has shifted away from this tragedy to everything that happened later in his life? If we want to start any relationship with the Prophet (pbuh) we have to start with the life of the lost little boy crying for his mother and a father that he never knew. Does your heart cry for this orphan? Do you want to take him in your arms and wipe his tears and tell him that you will hold his hand for as long as you live and never let it go? Why then have we broken our promise and let go of his hand? Love for that little boy should overwhelm us since every blessing we receive from Allah is a result of the gift that Allah showered on that little boy. This is the beginning of why he should be more beloved to us than our own children.

The little boy returned to his grandfather's house where he found protection and love. He grew up minding Abdul Muttalib's camels with only the stars in the heavens to keep him company out in the hot desert sands. Certainly, the desert taught him many things that shaped his personality. He soon came to be recognized by the whole tribe of Qureysh as the most honest and trustworthy of them all. He was given the title of "Al Ameen." Later, the poor shepherd boy found a close friend in Abu Bakr, who came from a well to do merchant family. The two established a bond of friendship that lasted to the very end of their lives. Abu Bakr's love for the Prophet (pbuh) is an example for all of us to follow when it comes to having a relationship with the Prophet (pbuh).

The little boy grew up to become a merchant responsible for managing trading caravans to Syria. He soon came to the notice of Khadija, a wealthy businesswoman in Mecca. She was so impressed with Muhammad's (pbuh) personality she offered herself in marriage to him. Now at twenty-five years of age, the Prophet gladly accepted. This was the first time he had a family of his own.

In the next fifteen years Khadija bore six children—four girls and two boys. Once again, tragedy struck the Prophet (pbuh) a double blow. Both of his boys died soon after birth. He had been denied a father and now he was denied a son, twice. While the presence of his beautiful daughters must have soothed his heart, I imagine he must have cried anew each time he buried his sons and it must have brought back the haunting vision of him burying his mother many years earlier. But the desert had taught him patience and perseverance. It taught him to search for the larger meaning of life and seek the hidden mysteries that had been obfuscated by the paganism and injustice of Mecca's elite circles.

Now in his thirties, the Prophet would retire to the cave of Hira to get away from Mecca and clear his mind. It was here that he received a message from angel Gabriel. Almighty God had chosen the Prophet to revive the message of his forefather Abraham (pbuh): there is only One God worthy of worship and to Him belongs everything that is in the Heaven and the Earth. It was Muhammad's (pbuh) responsibility to bring the message first to the Arabs and then spread it across the whole world. At first Muhammad (pbuh) was overwhelmed by the enormity of the task. But once the initial shock subsided, he devoted his heart and soul fully to his mission.

The first twelve years of his prophethood were spent trying to convince Meccans of the truth of Allah's message. During this time, he was subjected to ridicule, vilified, ostracized, and abused. The same people who had called him "Al Ameen" were now trying to kill him. With unwavering patience and perseverance Muhammad (pbuh) stuck to his mission even when further tragedy struck him with the passing of his beloved wife, Khadija, and his protector and uncle Abu Talib.

Unable to stop him, the chiefs of Quraysh offered Muhammad (pbuh) the wealth of all Arabia. The Prophet's answer was sublime: "Even if they put the Sun in one hand and the Moon in the other, I would not forsake this mission." This was the orphan boy who came from nothing. No father. No mother. No wealth, no position, and no one to even wipe his tears. How can any man not fall in love with the genuine sincerity of this man and his message? Although Khadija's family rallied to his cause, as did Abu Bakr's friends, many of the Prophet's own family rejected him. After twelve years of persecution, Muhammad (pbuh) migrated to Yathrib, when it had become quite clear that the Qureysh in Mecca had resolved to kill him.

In Yathrib (which was renamed Medina), the Prophet (pbuh) set about the task of creating the community of equality and justice as laid down by Allah in the Quran. For ten years this nascent community faced challenges of annihilation by large armies from Qureysh and elsewhere. Time and time again, the Muslim community faced overwhelming odds but successfully overcame them with the help of Allah and their undivided unity and love for the Prophet (pbuh). In many ways the Prophet (pbuh) was the glue that held everyone together.

While the community enjoyed success after success, the Prophet (pbuh) continued to face personal tragedies. He had to bury three of his four daughters, his beloved uncle Hamza, and many others very near and dear to him. Despite these difficulties, each tragedy brought him closer to Allah. Each person was a gift. Each brought him comfort or companionship in one-way or another. Towards the end of the Prophet's life, half of Arabia lay at his feet but the Prophet never changed. His humility and compassion touched the heart of everyone he came in contact with. He was always concerned for the welfare of those around him. The Prophet had emerged as the greatest leader in Arabia, and yet he often had no more than a few dates to eat for dinner. Even then, he shared these with any guest who entered his house. His kindness was legendary. He never raised his voice, always smiled, and never broke his word.

He transmitted the Quran to the people and explained many of the practical aspects of worship and how to deal with the challenges of life. What more can any one person offer humanity?

So how do we emulate the Prophet? We have to look at the lives of the companions that surrounded him and walk in their shoes. That is the only way we can get back to holding the hand of the little boy as he cried over his mother's grave and never, never let go. The Prophet (pbuh) has our hand firmly in his grasp, then why are we constantly trying to jerk our hand out of his?

While the later successes from the Prophet's (pbuh) life have inspired generations of Muslims, I have always found his earlier vulnerabilities much more inspiring. I can relate to my own feeling of vulnerability at a younger age when I as a child and young adult could not live up to the expectations of my parents. I'd like to think I drew inspiration from the Prophet's (pbuh) perseverance especially when the climb was steep and uphill. Thankfully, I was spared the tragedies that befell him, but in the back of my mind I always considered life to be an uncertain venture. This imbued me with a sense of humility that has colored my entire life. It has allowed me to see others around me as similarly vulnerable, and therefore they should be treated with gentleness and compassion, rather than arrogance and domination. Another constant in my life has been the realization that Allah has blessed me not because He gave me so much in life but that He spared me many of the overwhelming challenges that others have faced. From the very first time I read the translation of the Quran, there has been one dua that has stayed with me ever since.

"Our Lord, do not impose blame upon us if we have forgotten or erred. Our Lord, and lay not upon us a burden like that which You laid upon those before us. Our Lord, and burden us not with that which we have no ability to bear." (Surah Al Baqarah 2:286)

Among other lessons I learned from the Prophet's (pbuh) life was the value of patience. Allah took away so much from the Prophet (pbuh)—parents, children, spouses—yet the Prophet remained undeterred and achieved astounding success. His capacity to accept Allah's will reminds me of the story of Prophet Moses (pbuh) and Khidr from Surah Al Kahf. We often do not get the things we want most in life. Sometimes we see the meaning years later. Other times, the events seem inexplicable. Disappointment, despair, and regret are often natural reactions, but we must remember what Allah teaches us:

"But perhaps you hate a thing and it is good for you; and perhaps you love a thing and it is bad for you. And Allah Knows, while you know not." (Surah Al Baqarah 2:216)

The Prophet's life is the perfect example of Allah's grand plan. His "Adl" (justice) is absolute. What He takes away from you is balanced by what He bestows on you, and those who are accepting of His Will with patience and gratitude are doubly blessed. This is a hard lesson to learn except for those who study the Prophet's (pbuh) life and come to appreciate the way he moved with Allah's will. I find that Allah has blessed me in many more ways in what I received as compared to what I might have missed and this may be the influence that the Prophet's (pbuh) example had on me.

The Prophet's (pbuh) greatest attribute was his honesty and trustworthiness. He was "Al Ameen." This is the ultimate virtue we must develop in order to show our true love for the Prophet (pbuh). Over my lifetime, I have found that the fruits of honesty, truthfulness, and justice, to be more rewarding than any momentary gain by taking any other course. The latter will always end in regret and ultimate loss.

For all of these reasons, part of the daily dua I make to Allah is that on the Day of Resurrection, the Prophet (pbuh) might ask for me to be by his side in the company of his companions. May Allah accept this dua! Ameen.

4 | THE FIVE PILLARS

The example of the companions of the Prophet (pbuh) redefine the true five pillars of Islam – Imaan, Aqlaaq, Ibaadat, Ilm and Adl.

On the authority of Abu 'Abd al-Rahman 'Abdullah bin 'Umar bin al-Khattab, who said: I heard the Messenger of Allah, say:

"Islam has been built upon five things – on testifying that there is no god save Allah, and that Muhammad is His Messenger; on performing salah; on giving the zakah; on Hajj to the House; and on fasting during Ramadan." *(Bukhari & Muslim)*

This Hadith forms the basis of the oft-mentioned five pillars of Islam. Every Muslim child is taught these five pillars from the very first moment of their understanding and over time the concept of Islam has become so codified by these five pillars that Islam has become synonymous with these five obligatory injunctions. Does fulfilling these five elements make you a Muslim? The answer is clearly yes and no. Anyone who recites the Shahadah is considered a Muslim; however, a reading of the hadith says quite clearly that Islam is "built" on these five elements. The word "built on" is very crucial to understand. It clearly implies that this in itself does not complete the "Islamic personality" by itself. It can be the foundational basis for what it means to be a Muslim. However, a mistaken belief has taken hold of the Muslim mind that fulfilling these obligatory elements is enough to be a "good" Muslim. The real question is how many of us would want to move into a house with only pillars, but no walls, doors, windows, or even a roof?

These are just a means to an end and we make a vital mistake in thinking that the pillars represent the end all and be all of being a good Muslim and the larger we build the pillars we become more religious. At the same time a house without structural integrity requires pillars so that it is not blown away with the lightest of winds. So focus on just the pillars, five or ten or even a hundred is a fool's errand. The foundation or the pillars must be in keeping to the proportion of the house you build. The more magnificent the house you plan to build the more structural integrity you will need and therefore strong pillars. It is the same with the Islamic personality that we should all strive to develop.

What then is this Islamic house (personality) that the Prophet (pbuh) alluded to? Beyond its foundation, a house may have pillars that give it the strength, the walls and the roof that provides protection and functionality, the doors and windows that give it the livability and ventilation and the gardens that complete the full beauty and splendor of a complete habitat. In a similar light, we have to think in terms of a complete Islamic personality and not focus ninety percent of our effort on just one element. That is a recipe for failure. So, what are the elements of the Islamic personality (house) that we have to build?

I believe there are five essential elements to being a complete Muslim. In order, these are:

1. Imaan (foundation)
2. Ibaadat (pillars)
3. Aqlaaq (walls)
4. Ilm (roof)
5. Adl (doors and windows)

1. Imaan (belief)

Imaan consists of five elements: belief in Allah, belief in the Last Day, belief in the Angels, belief in the Book revealed by Allah and belief in the prophets sent by Allah as guidance to mankind.

"Believe in Allah and the Last Day, and the Angels, and the Book, and the Messengers." (Surah Al Baqarah 2:177).

Believing in the unseen Creator and a day of reckoning is fundamental to establishing a Muslim identity. The strength of this belief, (not only why you believe but also what you believe) determines the beauty and scale of the house you build. Just as you cannot build a ten-story house on a two-story foundation, you cannot build a full Islamic personality on a weak belief in your Lord and Creator. The house will only be supported by what your commitment is to it. Imaan is therefore the foundation on which our house will stand. If we build it of sand, we will pay the price both in this life and the hereafter. We have to build it strong with concrete and steel.

2. Ibaadat (worship)

Ibaadat consists of five elements: Shahadah (there is no god but Allah and Muhammad is the Prophet of Allah), Salaat (prayer), Zakat (obligatory giving), Hajj (pilgimage), and Sawm (fasting in the month of Ramadan). These are important and obligatory (fard) on every Muslim, but these are a personal function enjoined on us to keep our life mission in perspective. These are the internal pillars that give our house its strength. It keeps us focused on our relationship to Allah and the commitment we professed to Him in the Shahadah and restricts the distractions of the world around us. Just as the walls of a house keep the wind and the rain out of the house, our Ibadat keeps the ugly and sinful ways away from us. It is our protection but we must have the personality to protect. Remember that the five salat were not made obligatory until Me'raj (10th year) and fasting was not made obligatory until after the battle of Badr (15th year). Zakat and Hajj were made obligatory in the 19th year after the first revelations.

3. Aqlaaq (character)

Aqlaaq also consists of five elements: good deeds to your parents, to your family, to your neighbors, to your community and to humanity. Unfortunately, this critical element of Islam is the one that seems to be the least emphasized in our teaching of the religion. The greatest accomplishment of the Prophet (pbuh) was that he took a nation steeped in jahilliyah and transformed it into a nation of mercy, compassion, justice, unity, honesty and trust. Only after this transformation was the weight of the Quran fully revealed and entrusted to the Muslim ummah. Anyone who dishonored these attributes became a munafikheen (hypocrite) because this dishonored his creed of Imaan.

We focus so very much on the previous element of Ibadat when the Quran and Sunnah are replete with the most important elements: feeding the hungry, freeing a slave, taking care of the orphans, brotherhood, humility, patience, perseverance and gratitude.

The Prophet (pbuh) has said, "Visiting a sick person is better than a thousand prayers." Yet we often put the cart before the horse, giving precedence to our own selfish ends rather than caring first for others.

When you look at a beautiful house you admire the overall appearance, the façade, the gardens, the doors and windows. No one counts to see how many internal pillars there are. Similarly if Muslims wish to be seen as the best of humanity, they need to present their best external façade, which is represented by their Aqlaaq. **This was the Prophet's (pbuh) secret weapon in his conquest of Arabia and the world.**

4. Ilm (knowledge)

Ilm consists of: knowledge of Allah, the Quran, the Sunnah of the Prophet (pbuh), the world (physical and biological sciences), and knowledge of the unseen (research). This is a fundamental element of the human journey on Earth. You cannot have true Imaan if you do not have knowledge of the Creator. This gives us a certainty to our being, a certainty to our mission and a certainty to our destiny. The knowledge that Allah has a most beautiful treasure waiting for us in the next life should be a source of immeasurable happiness if we are truly Muslim. Allah has helped us achieve this task by giving us a treasure map in the form of the Quran. If we want the treasure, we better study the map as thoroughly as possible. He has also given us a guide in the form of our Prophet (pbuh), who has given us instructions on how to prepare for the journey (the Hadith and Sunnah). Beyond that we have to seek knowledge of the terrain, the tough challenges of life, by knowing the physical environment we live in (biological, physical and economic) that allows us to make our journey easier. Finally, we have to seek knowledge of the unknown by research and innovation that can help humanity overcome challenges that are unknown and make the journey a little easier without getting tripped up. This last is incumbent on us as Allah has decreed us as his vice-regent on Earth. Therefore, we bear responsibility for all that is on Earth and it is our task to make this a better place. Unfortunately, we have abdicated this responsibility and left it to the unbelievers to seek out new discoveries. Imagine if Muslims took on this task! Imagine the pace of discovery if we truly had Allah's mercy and help with us that others do not! We should be the leaders not the followers. The Prophet (pbuh) said, "The best of people is one from whom good accrues to humanity." So let us lead in establishing new knowledge.

5. Adl (Justice)

Adl consists of: jihad to conquer the ego, to be honest and trustworthy, fair in all dealings (personal and public), fight oppression, and set the example that attracts the hearts and minds of the disbelievers to the glories of Allah. Adl is the culmination of all of the previous four essential traits: Imaan, Aqlaaq, Ibaadat, and Ilm. It is the proof that is in the pudding.

Inscribed on the hilt of the Prophet's sword: 'Forgive him who wrongs you; join him who cuts you off; do good to him who does evil to you, and speak the truth although it be against yourself.'

The Prophet's (pbuh) life is the perfect example of Adl manifested in a human being. Those who followed after him were called the "Rashidoon," not because of their military conquests, but because of their practice of absolute justice, modeled specifically after the Prophet's (pbuh) example. The Quran says:

"O you who believe! Be you staunch in 'idalat, witnesses for Allah, even though it be against yourselves or (your) parents or (your) kindred, whether (the case be of) a rich man or a poor man, for Allah is nearer to both (than you are)." (Surah An-Nisa, 4:135)

Imagine life as an ocean that we have to cross to get to our final destination. To do this we need a boat. Our Imaan is the sturdy wood that we need to build the boat with. If the wood is weak, the boat will never survive the journey. Our Aqlaaq is the boat itself that we use to cross the seas. If we have holes in our boat, how far will we go? Our Ibaadat are the oars we use to propel the boat. If one or two are missing we will only go in circles without making any progress. Our Ilm is the knowledge of the stars that helps us navigate towards our destination and finally the Adl is the power we have in our hands and feet to row the boat forward and meet any and all challenges on the seas. These five essential elements make for a complete Islamic personality. There can be nothing that is clearer in terms of the essence of being a Muslim, for this is what Allah tasked us to achieve and modeled through the Prophet's (pbuh) example. We simply cannot limit our horizon to the five ritual "pillars" of ibaadat alone.

5 | IMAAN

The foundation of belief is the Knowledge and understanding of his Creator.

"There is no deity (worthy of worship) except Allah and Muhammad (pbuh) is His messenger." This is the central creed of Islam and is called the Kalimah. Every Muslim repeats this Kalimah many times during the day in his prayers and in the remembrance of God. The first part of the Kalimah (There is no deity worthy of worship except Allah) is as old as mankind itself and was first taught to Adam (pbuh) by Allah himself. Over the many centuries since, man has forgotten to recognize where he came from and who his Creator was. This has required God to periodically remind men through a succession of prophets. This was the same creed that Noah (pbuh) brought, the same as Abraham (pbuh), the same as Moses (pbuh), the same as Jesus (pbuh) and many others in between and finally Muhammad (pbuh). The last half of the Kalimah "and Muhammad (pbuh) is His messenger," is the completion of the story of Allah's religion to mankind given to the Prophet Muhammad (pbuh) through the Quran. Allah attests in the Quran:

"This day I have perfected for you your religion and completed My favor upon you and have approved for you Islam as religion." (Surah Al Maidah 5:3)

The literal translation of the word "Imaan" is "faith" or belief. The Kalimah is the foundational portal to the world of Islam. Every convert begins his journey in Islam by taking the Shahadah, which is reciting the Kalimah and believing in it with sincerity of heart.

The words of the Kalimah have profound significance, "There is no deity (worthy of worship) except Allah..."

On the surface this appears as a very simple statement yet it carries a powerful message. The arrangement of words in the Kalimah are very specific in the importance of their meaning. The difference between declaring, "I love you," and "I love no one but you," is vastly different. In saying that "I love you," you are describing your feelings. In saying that "I love no one but you" you are not just describing feelings but are making an exclusive relationship contract with another person. So it is with the Kalimah! In accepting the Kalimah as the nexus of his belief, a person enters into an exclusive contract with his Creator. "There is no god, but the one God" defines acceptance of "a way of life" prescribed by God and overrides a person's ego and any wishes and desires that might conflict with God's wishes for mankind. This is the beginning of a journey where this commitment to Allah will be tested and sometimes severely tested, but through His Mercy Allah has provided a road map of guidance through His prophets so that mankind can keep the covenant they make with Allah.

"And We have sent down to you the Book as clarification for all things and as guidance and mercy and good tidings for the Muslims." (Surah An-Nahl 16:89)

Over the millennia, man has managed to lose or pervert Allah's singular message. Hence each prophet He sends comes to reset mankind. The message given to the last of the prophets, Prophet Muhammad (pbuh), was the most complete and the one which will be preserved until the end of time (Al Maidah 5:3).

What does the Kalimah signify beyond the mere words? The Kalimah is not just a statement of words but a contract that one enters into with his Creator that encompasses all aspects of belief, behavior and worship. For mankind, this belief system is codified through the Quran and the Sunnah of the Prophet Muhammad (pbuh). Allah requires those who attest to the Kalimah to be fully aware of the history of creation, man's purpose on Earth, and his eventual fate. This therefore, encompasses absolute belief in the following five elements:

"Believe in Allah, the Last Day, the angels, the Book, and the prophets." (Surah Al Baqarah 2:177)

Belief in each element of this statement is profoundly important to understand the full scope of the contract one has entered into with Allah. The Quran tells the stories of those who believed, then disbelieved, and their fates in this world and the Hereafter. A critical element is the belief in the final judgment of the Last Day when man will be resurrected and judged on how well he fulfilled the contract when he took the Shahadah.

"And who believe in the Revelation sent to you, and sent before yiour time, and (in their hearts) have the assurance of the Hereafter." (Surah Al Baqarah 2:3)

"For those that have fulfilled their contract, Allah has promised an eternal life of peace, tranquility, and happiness. Those who reject Allah in this world, will receive appropriate punishment.

*..any who believe in Allah and the Last Day, and work righteous-
ness, shall have their reward with their Lord; on them shall be no
fear, nor shall they grieve." (Surah Al Baqarah 2:62)*

In this verse, Allah has made clear the three cardinal elements of
the contract: the surety of belief, the final judgment, and prescribed
way of life. This is what defines "Imaan" – the words of the Kalimah
and the way of life (Islam). This is in sharp contrast to the Jews, who
believe in a Creator, just as Muslims and Christians do, but do not
believe there is a Hereafter. Without a belief in the Hereafter, life on
this Earth is devoid of any meaning. Why believe in a Creator at all?
Similarly, in Christianity there is belief in the Hereafter but the final
reckoning is dependent on belief in Jesus Christ as Son of God and his
death and resurrection. Rewards in the Hereafter are not dependent
on any laws of God or your deeds and actions during your earthly lives.
In such a situation there is no boundary for social, ethical and moral
values. This again devalues the fundamental purpose for human life
on Earth. Those who reject God or find substitute deities have a totally
different challenge. Therefore in Islam, one finds a complete message
and guidance for the now and the Hereafter.

Islam, therefore, is the only way of life. Allah's command for man
to serve Him by leading a righteous life, caring for others with truth,
honesty, and justice, and meeting the challenges of this world with
patience and fortitude. The Hereafter is the ultimate goal but the path
to the Hereafter lies in navigating the temptations of this world and
resisting the urge to be swept away by the delights of the here and now
for a "promise" made by an unseen God.

*"Those who believe in the unseen and perform the prayer, and
expend of that we have provided them." (Surah Al Baqarah 2:3)*

The degree to which a person believes in this "guarantee" dictates
the depth of his Imaan, for the more convinced he is of its truth, the
more likely he is to fulfill the purpose for his creation.

While most Muslims consciously subscribe to the above belief system, life on Earth can be a messy proposition. There are all kinds of challenges that can severely test the faith and commitment of people, but in this is Allah's plan to separate the wheat from the chaff:

"Do you imagine that they will be left at ease because they say, we believe and will not be tested with affliction?

Lo! We tested those who were before you, thus Allah knows those who are sincere, and know those who feign."
(Surah Al Ankabut 29:2–3)

Those that recognize Allah's hand in their lives, in good and the bad times, can find a reason to make their bond with Allah (Imaan) stronger. The lives of the Companions amply attest to this. In spite of extreme hardships, they were enormously successful in this world and also in the Hereafter. That is the conviction born of true belief. True Imaan does not mean surrendering out of helplessness, but striving with perseverance and forbearance.

The bigger challenge mankind faces, however, comes from a desire for self-gratification, namely via wealth, position and power. Man easily forgets that the life of this world is short and temporary; whereas, the life of the Hereafter is eternal. Allah makes this clear in the Quran:

"Know that the life of this world is but amusement and diversion and adornment and boasting to one another and competition in increase of wealth and children…And what is the worldly life except the enjoyment of delusion." (Surah Al Hadid 57:20)

This is a stark choice man faces, day in and day out, in small ways and large. Does he put his own desires above those of Allah or vice-versa? Those who make the right choice will reap immense rewards in the Hereafter and for those who disregard Allah's guidance will face severe punishment.

"And whoever disobeys Allah and His Messenger and transgresses His limits – He will put him into the Fire to abide eternally therein, and he will have a humiliating punishment."
(Surah Al Nisa 4:14)

While Paradise and punishment represent two extremes, they represent for many Muslims the overwhelming basis of their Imaan. Fear of the Hereafter is a great motivating factor and is fostered by the vast majority of Ulema and imams at every Friday khutba (sermon). Islamic teaching of young children also focuses very much on Heaven and Hell. Hell is used as a tool to control children's behavior without realizing the psychological impact on children's minds. Islam takes on the mantle of a dark or a fearful religion. Is it any wonder why so many children, as they grow up, wander away from Islam? Those that stay in Islam, the religion becomes a transactional enterprise. The good that I do is to go to Heaven and the bad that I avoid is to escape from the punishment of Hell. Allah has disappeared from the equation except as a harsh judge. What a travesty of Islam! Islam came to give mankind the good news. Islam means "peace." People mistake this as peace in the world but in fact it is the peace of the heart that Islam alludes to as the first and the more important. Once again the words of the Quran given to Adam (pbuh), Abraham (pbuh) and all the other prophets:

"Any who believe in Allah and the Last Day, and work righteous-ness, shall have their reward with their Lord; on them shall be no fear, nor shall they grieve." *(Surah Al Baqarah 2:62)*

Therefore, Islam should be a happy religion for Allah has made an unequivocal promise of His blessing on Muslims who do their part and live up to His standards. A Muslim who achieves this level of certainty and conforms to it actually has found true peace and can be considered to have achieved a higher level of Imaan and is referred to as a Mumin. The difference between a Muslim (one who conforms to the basic tenants of Islam) and a Mumin is, therefore, the degree to which a person is happy in his spirituality for he is living a life as commanded by Allah and has yakheen (conviction) in Allah's promises. A Mumin can be described as follows as in the Quran:

"Righteousness is not that you turn your faces toward the East or the West, but [true] righteousness is [in] one who believes in Allah, the Last Day, the angels, the Book, and the prophets and gives wealth, in spite of love for it, to relatives, orphans, the needy, the traveler, those who ask [for help], and for freeing slaves; [and who] establishes prayer and gives zakah (obligatory charity); [those who] fulfill their promise when they promise; and [those who] are patient in poverty and ailment and during battle. Those are the ones who have been true, and it is those who are the righteous."
(Surah Al Baqarah 2:177)

The Prophet (pbuh) describes these people as one "who tasted Imaan, who is convinced that Allah is his Lord and Islam is his way of life and Muhammad is his prophet" (Bukhari, Muslim by Abbas). These are the ones who go above and beyond the routines of rituals and actively seek the pleasure of Allah by serving others and fulfilling Allah's command to make the world a better place than the one they inherited. In their actions, happiness comes to them in multiple ways. First that Allah is happy with them, secondly the pleasure of seeing the happiness in the faces of those they have helped, and finally the happiness of the rewards of the Hereafter. These are truly the blessed ones with whom Allah is well pleased.

There are also those special people who have transcended even the stage of the Mumin. These are the ones whose recognition and knowledge of Allah is heightened to a state of mind that they are consumed by the love of Allah and His messenger. The world no longer is viewed as a material entity. Their only desire is to be with Allah. The Prophet (pbuh) describes them as people "who practice their faith as if they see Allah." Even though this is not possible, their God- consciousness leaves them oblivious of the material world. The Quran describes them as:

"Say: Lo! my worship and my sacrifice and my living and my dying are for Allah, Lord of the Worlds." (Surah Al An'am, 6:162)

These are the exceptional people and called Muhsin and they have achieved the state called Ihsan. Allah calls them His friends. Few truly can achieve this state but all need to strive for the ultimate, otherwise what use is the struggle of this life? The hadith of the Prophet describes them as:

"One who loves for the sake of Allah alone, and hates for the sake of Allah alone, and whatever he gives is for the sake of Allah alone, and whatever he withholds is for the sake of Allah alone– indeed he perfects his Imaan." (Abu Dawood)

In another Hadith Qudsi (#25) narrated by Imam Bukhari, the Prophet (pbuh) said that Allah said:

"Whosoever shows enmity to someone devoted to Me, I shall be at war with him. My servant draws not near to Me with anything more loved by Me than the religious duties I have enjoined upon him, and

My servant continues to draw near to Me with supererogatory works so that I shall love him. When I love him I am his hearing with which he hears, his seeing with which he sees, his hand with which he strikes and his foot with which he walks. Were he to ask [something] of Me, I would surely give it to him, and were he to ask Me for refuge, I would surely grant him it. I do not hesitate about anything as much as I hesitate about [seizing] the soul of My faithful servant: he hates death and I hate hurting him."

Just remember that "God does not accept belief if it is not expressed in deeds, and does not accept deeds if they do not conform to belief (Hadith). *May Allah grant all Muslims the pleasure of His mercy, blessings and love. Ameen!*

6 | SALAH

Salah is the lifeline that keeps man connected to Allah through life.

One of the fundamental aspects of Islam is the requirement to pray (Salah). It is mentioned in the Quran numerous times (67+) and almost in one form or another, in most of the Surahs of the Quran.

"Indeed, I am Allah. There is no deity except Me, so worship Me and establish prayer for My remembrance. (Surah Ta Ha 20:14)

And establish prayer and give zakah and bow with those who bow [in worship and obedience]. (Surah Al Baqarah 2:43)

And seek help through patience and prayer, and indeed, it is diffi-cult except for the humbly submissive [to Allah]."
(Surah Al Baqarah 2:45)

"My Lord, make me an establisher of prayer, and [many] from my descendants. Our Lord, and accept my supplication." (Surah Ibrahim 14:40)

What exactly is "Salah?" While most English translations of the Quran use the word "prayer" for the word "Salah," the actual meaning of the word "Salah" is much broader. In Arabic the actual meaning of the word Salah is connection or communication. When using this definition, Salah or Salat takes on a whole new meaning. It is no longer a passive ritual, but an active form of a real dialogue. It is the difference between calling someone on the phone and leaving a message compared to having a meaningful conversation with the other party. Which would be more satisfying?

Salah has been a part of Allah's religion given to mankind through His many prophets from the beginning of time. The form of Salah may have taken different forms but as long as humans have recognized God they have prayed (communicated) in one way or another. Even those who just say "oh, God!" are praying/communicating with the Almighty.

While prayer was established early for Muslims, Allah decreed the five daily prayers on the occasion of Isra and Me'raj (ascension). While the exact date of this event is uncertain, it is said to have occurred a year before the Hijra (migration) placing it in the eleventh year after the initial revelation of the Quran.

Why was Salah revealed to the Prophet (pbuh) so late in his mission and not at the beginning if this was so important to Allah? In this is the crux of the issue of what Salah is all about. Early revelations came down to the Prophet (pbuh) to first prepare a community to (1) recognize that the Creator of the universe, the Almighty God, is the only one worthy of worship, and (2) to understand their true relationship and commitment to the Almighty. Those who accepted the religion of Islam had first to realign their hearts and minds away from the glamour and glitter of this world to one of service to Allah, specifically through service to fellow men. The early Muslims had to learn that sacrifice of personal ambitions was essential. Truth, kindness, and justice were paramount features of this new relationship. The hallmark of serving Allah could be found in caring for the needy, the orphan and the wayfarer. Worship is found in freeing slaves and putting the welfare of others before their own. Only after this realignment of the heart did Salah become meaningful. In effect Salah was not sent down as a ritual, but as an affirmation of the special relationship between a person and his Creator. The reason Salah was not foisted on Muslims early on, is because Allah was indicating that man must first become a Muslim in heart and mind before his Salah takes on real meaning.

Why is Salah prescribed five times a day? At the Me'raj, Allah ordered Muslims to pray fifty times a day, but in His infinite mercy, reduced the requirement to five times. These times of Salah are bio-synched to the cadence of human nature. Early in the morning, a man starts his day (Fajr) with a positive awareness of his Creator and Master. However, as the day advances, the world starts to override his awareness of Allah and so he is brought back to reality with the noon prayer. Then as the day advances, this reminder requires more frequent reinforcement (Asr and Magrib) as the temptations of the world also increase in frequency. Lastly the night prayer (Isha) is for accounting. It is to thank Allah for all the good things that he has received: his safety, his "risq" (provision), and the health and well-being of his family. Isha prayer is also designed to help review the day's events to make sure one has not transgressed Allah's commands by either omission or commission, and if so, to recognize these shortcomings and ask for forgiveness of Allah with a commitment to set a corrective course for the future. There are five questions every Muslim should contemplate after Isha Salah:

1. Have I thanked Allah?

2. Did I do anything dishonest?

3. Have I been unjust in my dealings with others today?

4. Have I hurt someone by my actions or my words?

5. Have I done something good today?

Answers to these questions and appropriate action will cleanse a person's heart and bring him peace, for it is only then that he will truly be in concordance with Allah's will.

But what actually is Salah? Many good people of strong religious beliefs often say "let us go and perform Salah," or, "it is time to perform Salah!" Salah is not a performance. At the beginning we said that Salah actually means communication or establishing a connection. It would therefore be more appropriate to say, "let us go and communicate with Allah." When you understand the words recited during Salah, you see that these words are actually a dialogue between a servant and his master. The core of formal Salah is Surah Al Fatiha, repeated at the beginning of every rakat. This critically important Surah is made up of three elements. The first part defines who this Salah is addressed to--the praiseworthy, the Lord of the World, the Merciful and the Compassionate, the Master of the Day of Judgment. This is how a person addresses a king in his court. During Salah we are in Allah's court. The sincerity of our praise determines how receptive the king (Allah) will be to what follows. The second part defines why we are standing in front of Allah at that moment. We have come to ask for His help because He is the only one we look to for help. The third part is where we present to Him our request for guidance that we may stay on the "straight path," the path that is defined by Allah and is pleasing to Him. While every Muslim may understand these elements of the request, what is often not recognized is that the "path" is just the means, just like any other road. What we have to focus on is not just the road but where we want the road to lead. The destination is far more important. **The entire purpose of Salah is to travel a safe "path" that leads us closer to Allah's Grace.** Islam is all about the destination, the destination, the destination! Prayer is a dialogue. It is a two-way communication, and Allah has assured us that when we ask anything of Him with true longing and sincerity, we will receive in abundance far more than what we asked for.

This cannot be said for one who performs the salah as an obligatory, boring, daily ritual.

After asking for forgiveness, the remainder of the prayer concludes with praise of Allah and sending blessings on the Prophet (pbuh). **The proof of how Allah has answered our supplication lies in how we experience life in between the prayers.** If we were truly sincere, we enjoy serenity, content and happiness. But if we were performing a mindless ritual we experience turmoil, doubt, uncertainty and unhappiness.

It is important to remember that our Creator (the One who knows us best) originally decreed fifty prayers for us. When the world is rushing by, it does not take long for man to be pulled away from the closeness he enjoys in Allah's court during the Salah. Therefore, during the times when one is not performing formal Salah, one can perform frequent dhikr (remembrance of Allah). This too is an effective form of communication with Allah. This prevents us from going through big swings in our consciousness of Allah during the day.

Allah asks us to come to Salah early during the scheduled times. You can imagine Allah's court as a "Darbar." Those that get in early, show eagerness, which is pleasing to Allah. They not only get the benefit of Allah's full attention but also His full blessings. Those that are tardy and come with some reluctance may not be so lucky, let alone those who do not even show up at all! Just like "Black Friday" shopping, the best deals go to those first in line!

So, we must be mindful of our Salah. We should, come early, come with sincerity, and come with a clear destination in mind.

In the very first revelation, Sure Alaq (96), Allah describes the beginnings of human life as that of a "clinging clot" in a mother's womb (Rehma- Arabic for womb). The clot needs the womb to survive and grow, but the womb does not need the "clot" for its well-being. It is through this attachment that the growing "clot" gets its nutrition and all its other needs. Similarly if Allah is our Rehma through whom all our needs are met, then Salah is the umbilical cord that keeps us firmly anchored to the source of all protection and sustenance. Sure Baqarah reads:

> *"Be guardians of your prayers, and of the midmost prayer, and stand up with devotion to Allah." (Sure Baqarah 2:238)*

The best way to imagine this is to think of an astronaut on a space walk. The astronaut is anchored to the space ship by a tether that keeps him attached, safe and provides vital oxygen. Imagine if this tether is severed, the astronaut will float away into a void and not survive. Who would deliberately ever sever this tether? Salat is that tether that keeps us attached to Allah and deliberately severing this lifeline has disastrous consequences. So be careful and regular in your salah and constantly stay connected to Allah.

7 | SAWM

Ramadan is the best of months because man has made Allah his first and only priority.

Fasting is an ancient custom that is a common feature of many religions. In recent times fasting has lost much of its spiritual connections and is much less practiced than in the past. In most religious communities, fasting was a communal activity, often tied to celebrations or significant religio-historic events. Nowadays, fasting is more commonly used for weight loss than spiritual refinement.

Fasting is most often said to induce discipline. In addition, it gives you a sense of appreciation for the less fortunate who have little access to adequate food and water. Then there are the health benefits. Recent studies from the University of Southern California have shown that fasting significantly improves brain function by releasing natural growth factors that enhance cognition and memory. It has also been shown to reduce neuro-degenerative diseases such as Parkinson's and Alzheimer's. Fasting also is reported to stimulate the immune system while also having significant anti-inflammatory effects. Fasting lowers the levels of IGF-1, a growth-factor hormone that has been linked to aging, tumor progression, and cancer risk. In modern secular culture fasting is being promoted as an important health benefit and there are now many recommendations for fasting of one kind or another. While intermittent fasting has become widely accepted in popular culture, the spiritual benefits remain unsung.

While fasting always has been a part of early and ancient religions, the form and degree of fasting varies substantially. Among the early pagan religions like Hinduism and Buddhism, fasting is not obligatory and the rules of fasting vary among different sects. Generally, the fast may involve eliminating one meal in the day (common) to abstaining from all food, but allow liquids (rare). Fasting was considered a moral and spiritual act where the aim was to purify the body and mind and acquire divine grace. Some popular days of fasting were the festivals of Purnima (full moon) and Ekadasi (the 11th day of the fortnight), Navratri, Shivratri and Karwa Chauth. Fasting became a popular form of political dissent in modern Hindu traditions after the civil disobedience campaigns of Mahatma Gandhi. Political prisoners have reverted to this practice on occasion when under severe duress.

Amongst the Abrahamic religions of Judaism and Islam fasting is an obligatory requirement. In the Old Testament there are several references (in the books of Samuel, Daniel, Ezra, Nehemiah, Psalms, and more) to the requirement of fasting:

"This is what the LORD Almighty says: "The fasts of the fourth, fifth, seventh and tenth months will become joyful and glad occasions and happy festivals for Judah. Therefore love truth and peace." — Zechariah 8:19

Fasting was required particularly on Yom Kippur, the Day of Atonement. This included desisting from eating or drinking, washing or bathing, marital relations, wearing leather shoes, and applying luxurious oils as a sign of repentance by denying oneself of basic needs. The fast lasts for 25 hours from sundown to the following sundown. There are twenty-five other days when fasting is required; most of these relate to major historical events such as the destruction of the first and second temple, commemorate other sacrifices, deaths, destructions, and sieges etc. Current practice is such that few Jews follow these requirements and only minorities of observant or orthodox Jews even keep the fast of Yon Kippur (<40% Pew Research).

In Christianity Lent is observed by Roman Catholics only and there is no fasting for Protestants. Christianity abrogated the Laws of the Old Testament and therefore fasting fell by the wayside. Lent falls around Easter and is in remembrance of Jesus's crucifixion and his resurrection. It begins on Ash Wednesday and ends on either Holy Thursday, Palm Saturday or Palm Sunday — depending on what you believe. The fast of Lent is a virtual fast with most people avoiding any one of their favorite things like chocolate, coffee, TV, or social media for the duration of Lent! Roman Catholics often mark their foreheads with ash as a "reminder that we are dust and to dust we will return." This type of fasting was not just to eliminate something from your life, but to supplement it with prayer.

In Islam fasting is very different and is an obligatory aspect of worship (ibaddat):

"O you who believe! Observing As-Sawm (the fasting) is prescribed for you as it was prescribed for those before you, that you may become Muttaqun (the pious)."
(Surah Al Baqarah 2:183)

This is a direct command from Allah and it came down in the second year after Hijra (Quranic year 14). Ramadan is the (month) in which was sent down the Quran as a guide to mankind, with clear signs for guidance and judgment (between right and wrong). (Surah Al Baqarah, 2:185)

Allah chose the ninth month of the lunar (Islamic) calendar, the month of Ramadan, as the prescribed month for fasting. This was the month when the Quran was first revealed and Allah has indicated that this is a month of very special mercies. The biggest blessing of Ramadan is that Allah has promised the believer that He will forgive all the sins of man if he comes to Allah with sincerity and commits to a life of piety, aqlaaq, charity and kindness. Many people are buoyed by the idea that past sins are forgiven, and while this is true, it also is conditional on future behavior.

Fasting in Ramadan is for each day of the whole thirty days of the month. The fast begins approximately an hour before sunrise and ends at sunset each day. Muslims are enjoined to eat (suhr) before they begin the fast and promptly break their fast at sundown (iftar). During the fast they are forbidden to eat or drink anything and to abstain from intimacy with their spouse. They are required to concentrate on their other obligatory worship and to give charity, be good to others and concentrate on their relationship to Allah.

There is no communal compulsion to fast and no one to observe whether a person is observing a fast or not. It is an individual exercise of one's will and desire. Food and drink are the most important of human urges beyond the fact that a person has to breathe to survive. A person will not forgo this strong an urge unless he loves someone or something more than he loves himself. By fasting, a person is making a statement about the priorities in his life. When fasting, a person becomes most conscious of his dutiful relationship with his Creator for whose command he is fasting. This heightened consciousness lifts his spiritual connection with his Creator and adds depth to the sincerity of his belief. This heightened consciousness also translates into all other acts of worship, i.e. prayer, alms giving, and the performance of other good deeds. When this happens, the fast becomes enjoyable rather than ritualistic. In fact, many people thrive in their self-deprivation. Speech is very much moderated. Self- assessment becomes necessary and leads to self-improvement and a sense of achievement. Sustaining this improvement through the months when fasting is not called for is then essential to fully reap the benefit of the fasts. All of these benefits only come from an understanding of why we fast. If not, a ritual cycle of fasting and gluttony becomes self-defeating because in subsequent months when fasting disappears, gluttony remains and is easily translated from food to other desires in life. Similar to the impact of meaningful prayer, fasting is not about what happens just in the month of Ramadan but how it affects your life in the other eleven months.

Ramadan also is the month wherein the Prophet (pbuh) said that all the gates to heaven are opened wide while the gates to Hell are closed. This is a metaphorical way of saying that during this month Allah's blessings are multiplied so enormously compared to other months that in the scale of Allah's mercy there is no limit to rewards for your good deeds. Why is Ramadan so special? When you look at all of the "Ibadat" (worship) that Muslims are required to do, all of them are designed to help Muslims stay focused on Allah's mission within a world of competing distractions. Interestingly, fasting (Sawm) is the one exception wherein the worship is a sacrifice and a gift that Muslims make for Allah. Allah's largesse and incalculable rewards are His way of thanking the believers.

While we focus on the rewards in the Hereafter, there are very significant benefits in this life as well. The decision to commit to fasting for one whole month is not easy. It comes only from great introspection of who we are, what our beliefs are, what our relationship is to Allah and how can we take this opportunity to build on this relationship. Unfortunately, in many places, people sometimes lose this opportunity by undertaking the fast as a passive cultural practice. In contrast, those who make an active decision to fast must make serious modifications from their normal daily life. These are the true believers. They make a commitment to the Quran, both to read and understand it. They make a commitment to their daily and supplemental prayers through focus and reflection. They make a commitment to charity over and above their norms. Most importantly, they sincerely try to fix their interpersonal relationships—a true measure of their success in Ramadan. The Quran says:

"Hurry towards your Lord's forgiveness and a Garden as wide as the heavens and the earth prepared for the righteous, who give, both in prosperity and adversity, who restrain their anger and pardon people—God loves those who do good." [Surah Al 'Imran, 133-4]

It is through these acts that people develop a far higher consciousness of Allah. It is not simply a matter of giving up food and water, but the overall change in lifestyle that pleases Allah. This is the overwhelming motivation of why Muslims fast. The potential rewards in the Hereafter are only an ancillary benefit. It is a well recognized fact, that it is in this month of Ramadan that Muslims worldwide are the happiest, most-satisfied, almost euphoric and congratulatory to one another. No one talks of difficulties or sufferings. What a blessing! It is for this beautiful state of mind that fully 80% of Muslims (Pew research) fast during Ramadan. In summary if one were asked to define the month of Ramadan, it would be called the month of HAPPINESS and JOY.

Many people believe the joy comes from personal accomplishment or on completing the task of fasting the whole month but the joy is really the feeling of real closeness to Allah during this month. Why then do we abandon this joy for the mundane feelings of worldly affairs during the rest of the year. Being a Muslim is being Happy and joyful the whole year because we are the only ones who have been promised Allah's mercy both in this world and the next. What more could we want and how lucky we are.

8 | ZAKAT

Zakat is not alms-giving but sharing your gifts from Allah with your less fortunate fellow men.

Zakat is an obligatory cornerstone of Islam. The importance of Zakat can be gauged by this verse in the Quran that says about the pagans:

"But if they repent, establish prayers, and practice zakat they are your brethren in faith." (Surah Tauba 9:5)

In a similar light, there is an authentic saying of the Prophet that tells us that not only are those who do not pay Zakat hypocrites, but that God will not accept their prayers as well. God's punishment for those who willfully refuse to pay Zakat will be severe on the Day of Judgment. The implication is that Zakat is a necessary part of belief.

"And woe to those who join gods with Allah– those who pay not Zakat." (Surah Fussilat 41:5)

What is "Zakat?" There are two basic meanings of the word. The first is "to thrive, to grow and to increase." The second meaning is "to purify." In the Quran, the word "Zakat" is applied to material items that a man possesses. It is a means of purifying your possessions and enjoying the dual benefits of Allah's pleasure in fulfilling your obligation to Him, and also seeking His Mercy, which multiplies your wealth in this world and the next. Unfortunately, we often see Zakat translated as "alms-giving." The idea of giving has become a psychological detriment in the minds of Muslims. The idea of giving always causes resistance in the human mind and you can see this even in infancy where a child's impulse is to hold on to his toys rather than share with siblings and others. The child who is generous in sharing is often well liked and is likely to receive many more gifts thereafter. This urge of possessiveness becomes much stronger as people get older and develop a feeling of entitlement for what they have "worked for."

"Zakat" should be redefined as "sharing" rather than "giving." It is only in this context that you can purify your remaining possessions and enjoy Allah's mercy. This is Allah's promise for those who truly believe.

A derivative of the word Zakat is "Tazkiah" where the same concept is applied to the purification of your heart:

"We have sent you a Messenger, from yourselves (Muhammad), reciting to you Our verses and purifying you (through Tazkiah) and teaching you the Book (Quran) and wisdom (Sunnah) and teaching you that which you knew not." [Surah Baqarah 2:151]

Again, there is nothing about giving in this verse. It is about receiving the knowledge and wisdom of the Quran and Sunnah to cleanse your heart of the many obstacles that stand in the way of purity and total commitment to Allah. Yes, Tazkiah requires you to give up on arrogance, greed, unlawful desires, lying, cheating, backbiting, etc., but this giving up is about rebalancing your inner self between your mind and your heart. Replacing these unholy urges in your heart with a desire to share with your fellow humans is the means and reward of purifying your heart.

"On that Day, neither wealth nor children will be of any benefit, only he (will be happy) who comes before Allah with a sound heart free of evil." (Surah Ash-Shu'ara 26:88).

This is what Allah told Adam when he sent him down to Earth:

"We did say, 'Down with you all from this [state],' there shull, none the less, most certainly come unto you guidance from Me: and those who follow My guidance need have no fear, and neither shall they grieve."- (Surah Al Baqarah 2:38)

The importance of Zakat can be seen by the fact that the word is mentioned eighty-two (82) times in the Quran. In contrast, the word "Salah" is mentioned sixty-seven (67) times, and the phrase "Salah and "Zakat" are mentioned together thirty-two (32) times in the Quran.

"Ta Sin. These are verses of the Quran- a book that makes things clear; A Guide and Glad tidings for the Believers- "Those who establish regular prayers and give Zakat (poor-due) and also have full assurance of the Hereafter." (Surah An Naml 27:1-3)

This verse encapsulates everything that Allah desires from us. In the Quran, every prophet was given similar instruction (7:156, 9:60, 19:31, 19:55, 21:73, 23:4, 27:3, 30:39, 31:4 and 41:7). In essence, this is a covenant between Allah and the Believers that was given to Adam and every prophet that was sent after him. The requirement of Zakat was revealed in Medina to Prophet Muhammad (pbuh) in the second year after Hijra (14th Quranic year). Since then the requirement of Zakat has become a foundational pillar of Islam. In fact, after the death of the Prophet (pbuh) many newly converted tribes of Arabia resisted the payment of Zakat. The Caliph (successor) Hadrat Abu Bakr declared war on every group who resisted the payment of Zakat (Ridda wars) until all had been brought back into alignment with the dictates of the Quran and instructions of the Prophet (pbuh).

The rules of Zakat are generally mentioned in the Quran, yet as the world has evolved it has raised interpretive differences about how to calculate Zakat, who is eligible to receive Zakat, and how Zakat funds should be best utilized. The subject is also complicated by a fairly large collection of Hadith where we see entire books dedicated to the subject (i.e. Sahih Bukhari (24), Sahih Muslim (5), and Sunan Abu-Dawud (9)).

Who has to pay Zakat? As we have seen above, Zakat is compulsory for every Muslim who has accumulated material wealth above a base amount (nisab), which is usually equivalent to 3 oz. of gold. Material wealth includes gold, silver, cattle, crops, investments, savings, etc. that a person has owned for an entire prior year. Zakat is exempt on personal use items such as houses, cars, furniture, clothes, etc. Generally, the minimum amounts of Zakat according to the Hadith of the Prophet (pbuh) is 2.5% on static investments and 5-20% on the investment income of appreciating assets like crops, etc. With so many different types of instruments in the modern world it has become a matter of constant review by various Fiqh councils across the world and it may be most appropriate to follow their guidelines. Allah says in the Quran:

"They ask you," O Prophet, what part of their wealth they should spend charitably. Say: "Spend of your "surplus wealth."
(Surah Al Baqarah, 2:219).

Allah has also defined in Surah Tauba (9:60) rules as to who can receive Zakat. These include fuqara (needy), masakin (poor), amilin alaiha (the manager of Zakat), muallafat ul qulub (the person who newly converted to Islam), fir riqab (freed slaves), gharimin (people who owe), fi sabilillah (in Allah's way), and ibn us sabil (travellers). While most of these categories are clear, scholars, do include any and all activities in support of Islam in the category of "fi sabilillah." This also has led to many controversies about whether you can use Zakat funds to build or support Islamic schools, masjids, etc. that also benefit the Muslim community. The guidance of Allah comes as a Mercy to mankind and therefore it is far more important what lies in the heart of the person sharing his wealth "in the cause of Allah (fi sabilillah") than rigidity of any rules of interpretation. That being said, Zakat cannot be given to lineal antecedents or descendants (parents and children). Zakat can, however, be given to needy siblings and other relatives.

Why is Zakat so important in Islam? Many scholars have enumerated a variety of reasons.. These include economic redistribution of wealth, a rebalancing of economic activity in an Islamic community, social welfare, reduction of beggary, crime, and the exploitation of the weaker segments of society, etc. All of these reasons and many more are valid and all look at Zakat from the perspective of the recipient. **However, the main purpose of Zakat is to benefit the giver more than the recipient.**

One of the cardinal attributes of Allah is His Mercy (ar-Rehman, ar-Raheem). Though His Mercy encompasses all human beings, He has materially favored some more than others. When Allah asks a believer to share the gifts of His Mercy, He is asking him to manifest the same mercy to others that was bestowed on him. If you exemplify Allah's generosity in this world, He will be generous with you many times over in the next. Conversely, if you are tight-fisted in this world, why should Allah be generous with you in the next? It is only when you meet your obligations fully and magnanimously have you purified your heart as well as your wealth. This is the fundamental reason for Zakat. The societal benefits are secondary.

The practical economic benefits of Zakat to the Muslim ummah can be astronomical if all Muslims are vested in the practice, and if the Zakat funds are distributed appropriately. It is estimated that the global zakat contribution world-wide could amount to $200 billion per year. This amount is considerably larger than the total aid spent by all countries! However, the naked facts remain that poverty, illiteracy, and worsening health keep rising in Islamic majority countries decade after decade.

A fundamental rethinking is required in matters of effective Zakat utilization. Muslims make up 24% of the world population but 50% of those below the poverty line. There are numerous suggestions on how to effect change but implementation seems to be a real problem at the governmental level. Of the several countries that have mandated a centralized collection of Zakat, most are unsuccessful at collecting adequate sums because individuals feel that they can be more effective in deploying their charity.

In the early years of Islam, Zakat was collected centrally by the Caliph and redistributed appropriately. However, during the time of Hadrat Uthman, this practice was eliminated, as there were no eligible recipients for Zakat in Medina. Attempts to centralize this again have had variable results. It should therefore become an overriding objective of the Muslim Ummah to raise the community out of the sinkhole of poverty that we find ourselves in. A truly successful Zakat fund should not only feed the poor, but give them the tools to rise out of poverty.

9 | HAJJ

Hajj is not the visit to the Kaaba but it is time spent at Arafat in contemplation, introspection, and dua.

The Hajj is the last of the five pillars of Ibaadat in Islam. Every Muslim has a deep desire to perform this ritual and for those who are lucky enough to accomplish this task, it has a lasting significance. Unfortunately, this significance is not always spiritual. In earlier days many people used the completion of hajj as a status symbol and attached the prefix of "Hajji" to their name. It was an understandable phenomenon in a time when the journey was difficult (often dangerous) and required a significant financial investment. Nowadays, the journey has become considerably easier, safer, and far more comfortable. This has enabled many more people to perform Hajj, not once, but many times over. While the sincerity of people should not be doubted, it certainly gives pause to consider if the overriding significance of the Hajj is becoming lost.

The literal meaning of the word "hajj" is to go on "a journey to a place." As mentioned in the Quran, this place is the "Kaaba" in Mecca, during the lunar month of Dhul-Hijjah.

> *"The most important shrine established for the people is the one in Becca; a blessed beacon for all the people."*
> *(Surah Al Imran 3:96–97)*

The pilgrimage is performed over five to six days from the eight to the thirteenth of the month. The rites of the Hajj are fairly basic and include pronouncing one's intention, putting on the Ihram, visiting the Kaaba to perform Umrah, and then proceeding to Mina. After remaining in Mina for three days, pilgrims then proceed to the plain of Arafat until 'Asr prayer, and then travel to Muzdalifah to spend the night. They then return to Mina to stone the three pillars representing Shaitan, and sacrifice an animal to celebrate the day of Eid. Upon completion of the sacrifice, pilgrims finally proceed back to the Kaaba to perform a farewell Tawaf (seven counter clock-wise circumambulations), Sa'i (brisk walk between the hills of Safa and Marwa), and for men, shaving of some or all of the hair on their head. Of all of these rituals, the most important moment of Hajj is the time spent at Arafat in prayer and contemplation.

What really is the significance of Hajj? Hajj is the ultimate testament of a Muslim's commitment and service to his Creator. It is mentioned that Allah established the sacred site of the Kaaba when the Earth was formed. However, it is the journey of our ancestor Abraham (pbuh) who grew up in a sea of paganism, that brought humanity back to Allah –the one and only true God. With him we see the creed of Islam- "there is no God but the One God and He only is worthy of worship." The story of Abraham (pbuh) is well known to us. His firstborn son, Ishmael (pbuh) was born to Abraham (pbuh) and Haggar (ra) when Abraham (pbuh) was eighty-six years old in the land of Canaan. Allah asked Abraham (pbuh) to take Haggar (ra) and the baby to the far-off barren desert valley of Mecca and leave them there all alone amongst all the dangers of the desert. Such was Abraham's (pbuh) commitment to Allah that he did as asked without fear, regret, or concern. Allah protected and provided for Haggar (ra) and the baby as evidenced by the well of Zamzam that flows with water even to this day some 3000-4000 years later. Abraham (pbuh) subsequently visited the valley of Mecca often and watched his son grow up. Abraham's example shows us the deep and ultimate connection that can be established between man and his Creator. Through developing that connection, we see God's promise to Adam (pbuh):

"Get you down all from here: and if, as is sure, there comes to you guidance from me, and whoever follows My guidance, on them will be no fear, nor will they grieve." (Surah Al Baqarah 2:38)

In the actions of Abraham (pbuh) we find the truth of Allah's promise. Those who profess to follow Abraham (pbuh) and the line of Allah's prophets until Muhammad (pbuh), follow the true creed of Islam. If you want what Abraham (pbuh) and the Prophets had, then you have to let go of any belief in your own self-sufficiency. You must surrender yourself wholly and completely with an unquestioning belief that Allah is the ultimate provider, sustainer, and protector. This is the reason for the Hajj. Clearly it is more than a journey to Mecca. It is a journey of life. It is a journey to Allah and until this realization and recognition is embedded in your heart the journey will remain incomplete.

Allah has placed great emphasis on the Hajj in the Quran. There is a whole chapter of the Quran (22) devoted to the Hajj and there are many other verses (Quran 2:125, 2:158, 2:189, 2:196, 2: 197-198, 2:200-3, 3:96-7, 5:1-2, 5:94-96, 9:2, 9:36-7, 48:27) that define the rules and rituals for performing Hajj. Most of these are as performed by Prophet Abraham (pbuh) after he and Ishmael (pbuh) had first built the Kaaba and installed the "Black Stone" into the walls of the cuboid structure.

"And proclaim that the people shall observe Hajj pilgrimage. They will come to you walking or riding on various exhausted (means of transportation). They will come from the farthest locations."

(Surah Al Hajj 22:27)

The rituals of Abraham's (pbuh) Hajj have been continuously been performed at the Kaaba ever since, even during the days of Jahilliya and pagan worship. It was under the guidance of the Quran and the Prophet Muhammad (pbuh) that many innovated and often perverted rituals (like performing Tawaaf without clothes, etc.), were cleaned up and the correct methodology for performing Hajj was codified for Muslims. Muslims also perform the sacrifice of an animal in remembrance of another challenge Allah asked of Abraham (pbuh): to sacrifice his first born son. Ishmael was the treasure of his father's heart. But at nearly one hundred years old, Abraham (pbuh) was willing to sacrifice his ultimate possession if Allah commanded it. None of us will ever reach the level of Taqwa (mindfulness of Allah) that Abraham (pbuh) or Ishmael (pbuh) attained, but it should prompt us to consider the value we place on our prized worldly possessions in contrast to the love we have for our Creator.

The day of Arafat on the tenth day of Dhul-Hijjah is recognized as the most significant rite of the Hajj. It begins soon after Fajr Salat when the pilgrims proceed from Mina to the plain of Arafat and stay at least until noon. The pilgrims then sit in contemplation and prayer, thinking of this journey and making the resolutions that will significantly impact their lives going forward.

Contemplation is the most important element of Hajj. It is the opportunity for a person to take stock of himself. Who has he become? Is he a person that the Prophet (pbuh) would approve of? Is he a person who is obedient to Allah and His commands? Is he a person who has made a whole-hearted commitment to the words of the Quran? Is he a person worthy of Allah's love and blessings? Certainly, everyone will find that he is deficient and can become a better person. At Hajj, he has to think about how to take the next step, and how he will need Allah's help for the next phase of his journey. This is where his prayers of sincerity come in.

Active introspection is far more powerful than performing a hundred ritual "salats." What meaning do they have? Of course, Surah Al Fatiha is the ultimate dua when it comes from the heart: "you are the only one we worship and you are the only one we ask for help." But when we recall the story of Hajjira (ra) and the infant Ishmael (pbuh) who were alone and desperate in the deserted valley of Mecca, we see that Allah's help came only after they had reached severe pangs of hunger and thirst. Similarly, Allah's help will only come when a pilgrim recognizes his spiritual deficit and suffers from spiritual hunger just as his forefather, Ishmael (pbuh).

To be sure, Allah never abandons those who sincerely call on Him in distress. We see this during the Battle of Badr, when the fledgling Muslim community reached out to Allah for help. In response, He unleashed an army of angels to help the believers, just as He provided the gushing well of Zamzam long before.

If we truly want Allah's help, we have to experience a spiritual hunger that purifies our call. Often we make the mistake of thinking that after we ask for Allah's help, we simply wait for something to happen. In reality, Allah is waiting for us. We need to take the first step and narrow the distance to Allah, if His full help and blessings are to reach us.

For those who complete the Hajj, Allah has made a promise: "Whoever performs Hajj and does not commit any obscenity or transgression will return [free from sins] as he was on the day his mother gave birth to him." (Bukhari)

The great significance of Arafat is also highlighted by the last and only Hajj that the Prophet (pbuh) performed, wherein he delivered his greatest manifesto—The Farewell Sermon:

"O People, listen well to my words, for I do not know whether, after this year, I shall ever be among you again. Therefore, listen to what I am saying to you very carefully and take these words to those

who could not be present here today.

O People, just as you regard this month, this day, this city as Sacred, so regard the life and property of every Muslim as a sacred trust. Return the goods entrusted to you to their rightful owners. Treat others justly so that no one would be unjust to you. Remember that you will indeed meet your LORD, and that HE will indeed reckon your deeds. God has forbidden you to take usury (riba), therefore all riba obligation shall henceforth be waived. Your capital, however, is yours to keep. You will neither inflict nor suffer inequity. God has judged that there shall be no riba and that all the riba due to `Abbas ibn `Abd al Muttalib shall henceforth be waived.

Every right arising out of homicide and blood-killing in pre-Islamic days is henceforth waived and the first such right that I waive is that arising from the murder of Rabi` ah ibn al Harith ibn `Abd al Muttalib.

O people, the Unbelievers indulge in tampering with the calendar in order to make permissible that which God forbade, and to forbid that which God has made permissible. With God the months are 12 in number. Four of them are sacred, three of these are successive and one occurs singly between the months of Jumada and Sha` ban. Beware of the devil, for the safety of your religion. He has lost all hope that he will ever be able to lead you astray in big things, so beware of following him in small things.

O People, it is true that you have certain rights over your women, but they also have rights over you. Remember that you have taken them as your wives only under God's trust and with His permis-

sion. If they abide by your right then to them belongs the right to be fed and clothed in kindness. Treat your women well and be kind to them, for they are your partners and committed helpers. It is your right and they do not make friends with anyone of whom you do not approve, as well as never to be unchaste...

O People, listen to me in earnest, worship God (The One Creator of the Universe), perform your five daily prayers (Salah), fast during the month of Ramadan, and give your financial obligation (zakah) of your wealth. Perform Hajj if you can afford to.

All mankind is from Adam and Eve. An Arab has no superiority over a non-Arab nor a non-Arab has any superiority over an Arab; also a white has no superiority over a black nor a black has any superiority over white except by piety and good action. Learn that every Muslim is a brother to every Muslim and that the Muslims constitute one brotherhood. Nothing shall be legitimate to a Muslim, which belongs to a fellow Muslim unless it was given freely and willingly. Do not, therefore, do injustice to yourselves.

Remember, one day you will appear before God (The Creator) and you will answer for your deeds. So beware, do not stray from the path of righteousness after I am gone.

O People, no prophet or messenger will come after me and no new faith will be born. Reason well, therefore, O People, and understand words, which I convey to you. I am leaving you with the Book of God (the Quran) and my Sunnah (the life style and the behavioral mode of the Prophet). If you follow them you will never go astray.

All those who listen to me shall pass on my words to others and those to others again; and may the last ones understand my words better than those who listen to me directly. Be my witness O God, that I have conveyed your message to your people."

This was the Prophet's (pbuh) farewell sermon delivered from Mount Arafat to all who were present testifying to the completion of the Prophet's (pbuh) mission and charging the Muslims present and who follow, to keep fidelity to the Quran and his example.

The plains of Arafat not only resonated with the Prophet's words, but also with what are believed to be the final verses to be revealed to the Prophet:

"This day I have perfected for you your religion and completed My favor upon you and have approved for you Islam as religion."
(Surah al Ma'idah 5:3)

The Day of Arafat was a day of completion. Allah completed the religion of Islam for us. The Prophet (pbuh) completed his mission in conveying the Message. The question remains, have we completed our mission? Let not the physical distance of Mecca or the distant month of Dhul-Hijjah stop us from fulfilling the spiritual journey every single day, of every single month, of every single year of our lives!

Just as we are required to spend our time in contemplation on the plain of Arafat, we need to spend time every day in contemplation even if it is for five, ten, or twenty minutes thinking of our place in Allah's grand plan and whether we are living up to our obligations.

10 | EARLY ISLAMIC EDUCATION

*Start young and focus on what is most important —
building character.*

Islamic education is often interpreted as teaching the Quran,
Sunnah and rituals of Ibadat (worship). Traditional priorities include
memorization and tajweed (proper pronunciation), as these are required to some extent to perform and lead the salah (prayer). Often the
goal of early Islamic education is considered to be the full memorization of the Quran (Hifz).

Over the last several centuries this approach has been the mainstay
of Islamic education and has provided a modicum of success in maintaining the preservation of Islamic theology and practice. Despite the
fact that Islam is fundamentally based on peace and justice, it appears
as though the dynamism of the faith has been lost in modern times.
Muslims today are a far cry from the Muslims who were the best of
people--the companions of the Prophet (pbuh). What is so different
between people of today and the companions of the Prophet (pbuh)?
What are we missing? Today's Muslims have economic well-being,
are far more technologically advanced, and have more academic tools

at their disposal. In contrast, the companions of the Prophet (pbuh) came from a background of Jahiliya. Most did not know about the one true God. Few could read and write. They were consumed with a hard pastoral desert life, where survival was often more important than religion. So how did the Prophet (pbuh) turn such people into the most admired and revered of all people? The answer is EDUCATION!

The Prophet (pbuh) did not start with preaching to his people about the Quran and Sunnah. Nor did he emphasize how to pray and fast. First he taught them how to be REAL MEN. What do real men do? They believe in Allah as the One and only true God and practice SOCIAL JUSTICE--to care for the welfare of fellow believers. No wonder the Prophet (pbuh) said:

"No one is a true believer until he desires for his/her brother that which he desires for himself." (Bukhari, Muslim)

Also Ibn Abbas reported, "The Prophet, peace and blessings be upon him, said, 'He is not a believer whose stomach is filled while the neighbor to his side goes hungry.'"

Although many of us think of education as a childhood endeavor, the Prophet (pbuh) was consumed with teaching adults. Similarly, we too should consider that the first way to influence children is to educate adults first. The first twelve years of revelation were devoted to the refinement of adult character. The transformation of the Muslims in Mecca so affected the hearts and minds of others that once Islam was established in Medina, many individuals and whole tribes rushed into the fold of Islam. Interestingly, the Prophet (pbuh) did not just teach this by words but through example. The more time the companions spent with the Prophet (pbuh), the more firmly they adopted the principles of social equality and justice. This is called "tarbiyah," the teaching of Islamic behavior as the first principle of Islam. The Quran stresses this point in Surah Al-Imran:

"By no means shall you attain righteousness unless you give (freely) of that which you love; and whatever ye give, of a truth God knows it well." (Al Imran 3:92)

They say the best way of teaching others is to first learn yourself. In the case of Islam, the best way to educate our children is to practice Islam as taught to the companions. A lifetime of education can be passed down to our children if only they see us actively caring for others in our community by sharing our wealth, time, and effort.

Islamic education can be classified under 3 categories.

1. Early (0 to 10-12 years)

2. Adult (12-40 years)

3. Legacy years (40+)

General principles of formal early Islamic education:

Early education starts not in Islamic schools, but in the home. Parents should spend maximum time playing with children not just when they are cute infants, but especially as they are growing up. It is during these playtimes that the best teaching opportunities arise. These are the times when children's minds are most receptive to your words and actions because these are happy moments when children are least reactionary. In addition, there are also a number of Islamic games on the market that parents can make full use of.

1. Allah

As early as possible, start familiarizing children with the names of Allah and teaching them basic "duas." The one element to avoid is the discussion of Heaven and Hell. Children should not be frightened nor should they develop a view of religion as a transactional process of rewards and punishment. In the house it is very important that the entire family prays together. Adults should make it a habit of not rolling up the prayer mat immediately after the prayer has ended but sit with their children and discuss or sing Allah's attributes. In the earliest phase, it is critical to help children develop a healthy relationship with Allah.

2. Sunnah

Stories of the Prophet (pbuh) need to be an everyday occurrence. In fact, much of the Quran is filled with stories of earlier prophets as a way of teaching Prophet Muhammad (pbuh) and the companions. From an early age, emphasis must be placed on stories of the Prophet's personality and his character. This includes stories of the Prophet's (pbuh) soft speech and avoidance of harsh words, stories of his smiling temperament, his non-judgmental attitude, his fairness in his dealing with others, and his sacrifices for his followers. When children make mistakes or misbehave, instead of scolding them that their mother or father will be angry, it may be more appropriate to tell them that the Prophet (pbuh) would not like their behavior.

3. Sharing

While children learn much of their behavior patterns by observing their parents, modern family life actually causes disconnect between family members. More time is spent in watching television than in shared experiences with children. An old maxim is that "the family that eats together stays together." What if half the family is watching TV while eating? Mealtimes are the most opportune moments for educating children. This is the time to share stories, teach proper manners and etiquette, and develop a spirit of sharing. Unfortunately, we have discarded a common eating custom from the early years of Islam. During the Prophet's time, a meal was shared from a single plate of food. Naturally, all those at the table learned to look out for each other.

Today people would consider this practice barbaric or unhygienic, but the moral value and the lesson of sharing far outweighs any such considerations. While today we may not want to go back to sharing the whole meal from a single plate, it is very important that we share some part of the food from a single plate. Sharing with others has to become second nature of the Muslim psyche. We have to eliminate the modern culture of "I" and "mine" from the Islamic lexicon and replace it with "we" and "us."   Aside from sharing meals it might also be helpful to make sure children have a smaller living space where the family must learn to get along and equitably share resources.

4. Community:

One of the unfortunate byproducts of modern life is that people exclusively make friends amongst their social and economic peers. This can create a social bubble wherein the children develop a very narrow view of the world. It is important to get to know and interact with less privileged families, and in fact, adopt them as the closest of friends. This also allows the adults to remain grounded in the real world rather than living in the clouds. Such behavior follows the tradition of the Prophet (pbuh) who spent more time among those who were less fortunate than himself. More often than not, these relationships tend to blossom into the truest friendships.

5. Giving:

It has become the norm to celebrate birthdays, graduations, Mother's Day, even Valentine's Day, by receiving gifts and cards. Most of the time the pleasure one receives is ephemeral and lasts no more than an hour or a day. Instead children and adults need to look at these as an opportunity for gratitude to Allah for the blessings He has showered on us. In response we should look at these as an opportunity to give to others rather than to receive. The pleasure of giving lasts considerably longer and is more fulfilling than the pleasure of receiving. Gifts should be given at Eid when Allah is also part of the celebration.

6. The Quran

Emphasis and understanding of Surah Ikhlas and Surah Al Fatiha must become second nature to children before they begin their journey into reading and memorizing the rest of the Quran. Learning the language and the correct pronunciation of words is important but should not be an all-encompassing effort. Some children are good with languages and have the ability to pick up these skills. Others have great difficulty and may need to take a different route to learning. In this light, we should not compare children across the board by the same educational standards when Allah has blessed each child with their unique abilities and challenges. It may be better to teach children to learn the Arabic language than rote memorization of the Quran for they may be able to communicate better with Allah during their salah.

7. Do's and Do not's:

Islamic rules of "Halal" and "Haram" should be introduced gently as children grow. None of these rules should be used to censure children. They should feel a commitment to these rules out of a sincere love of pleasing Allah. They should understand that these rules are there for our protection, not to deprive us of enjoyment.

When it comes to Islamic education, one thing can be said for sure: the behavior of parents has the greatest impact on their children. At the very least, parents must live by the same values they expect from their children. You simply cannot expect your child to be truthful if you are not!

11 | ADULT ISLAMIC EDUCATION

Gaining knowledge and giving of oneself is the practical side of Islam.

Adult Islamic education can be categorized by three elements – Self-Assessment, Knowledge, and "Tazkiah" (purification).

1. Self-Assessment

Entering adulthood is a very critical period in a person's development. It is also a period of considerable stress. There is a great deal of peer influence outside the home. A person starts to see the world very differently as his dependence on parental support dwindles. There is the stress of competing with others, early-on in school, then later in his chosen profession. During all of these sub-stages of adult development it is important to remember a few key questions: Who am I? What am I struggling toward?

Who am I? As humans, we have to realize that we are an infinitesimally small element in the universe. We are no more than a grain of sand on the shore of time that gets washed away, often without leaving a mark. True self-assessment begins with this humbling realization. Unfortunately, many people narrow the scope of the universe to their immediate surroundings such as their home, their work, or even their community or country. When their universe is limited to the people around them, it can set them up for a very egocentric approach to life. "You can be whatever you want to be," is the common slogan. This puts man at the center of his universe rather than God.

The one who falls in love with himself is the most deluded of all creations. This is the height of "kufr" (one who hides the truth). However much power or status he can achieve, it is nothing compared to Allah's power. For Ayatul Kursi tells us that He is "the Creator of all the Heavens and the Earth and everything in between." In this light, self-reflection is the way to rebalance the relationship between man and his Creator.

If the whole Universe were limited to our planet, man would be no more than an ant on it. His civilization would be no more than a colony of ants. What power does an individual ant have? It can be crushed in a fraction of a second by any number of forces around it. In reality "man" is no different for his power (even his life!) can be extinguished in an instant.

Each ant in a colony performs a vital function that sustains and grows the colony. Between the Queen and the worker ants, there are those that take care of the eggs, those that clean the colony, those that feed the larvae, and those that leave the colony to forage for food. Similarly, men provide a variety of different functions to sustain the human colony. Unlike ants that are preprogrammed to perform certain functions, men have to develop their skills and make choices. The success of these choices often leads men astray in thinking that they are superior to others who are less successful. Just as an ant cannot leave his assigned position in the ant colony, man must also stay in the lane of his prescribed function, namely to acquire knowledge (and skills) to support his community, to balance his relationship with his Creator, and to purify his heart by his actions.

How does a man come to this realization? It is a fundamental truth that however good we might be at any one thing; there are a multitude of things that we struggle with. Michael Jordan was the very best at basketball but struggled with baseball. Similarly, you may be a great doctor but a poor cook, a great scholar but a poor father, a great singer but a poor husband and so on. Like a successful ant colony, it is not your individual greatness that should define you but the cumulative greatness of all that surround you.

In my own case growing up, I was the black sheep of the family when it came to education. My dyslexia went unrecognized for quite some time. In contrast, my social awareness and general world view was much better than others. Even at a young age, many organizational tasks came much more easily to me than my siblings, and so my family came to rely on me for many tasks including care of my elder siblings. Nonetheless, during my later childhood years I often wondered why I could not be more like the others who were often admired and praised for the very skills I lacked. Years later, it slowly dawned on me that those who were admired and those who did the admiring both tended to depend on me more than I previously realized. It was this realization that helped me understand the value I brought to my "colony." This self-realization taught me that Allah had charted out a different lane for each of us. There is no need to compete with others, but to excel in our defined lane. This does not mean we give up on the challenges that do not play to our strengths. To be sure, I still had to deal with my educational shortcomings, as they would affect my future economic wellbeing.

Often when I faced a serious test my mother would send me off with two duas from the Quran. The first was the dua of Prophet Musa (pbuh), when Allah sent him to preach to the Pharaoh. Prophet Musa (pbuh) was well-aware of his speech impediment and famously called out to his Lord:

"Rabbish rahli sadri wa yassirli amri!

My Lord, expand for me my breast [with assurance] and ease for me my task, and remove the impediment from my tongue, so people may understand my speech." (Surah Ta-Ha 20:25)

The second dua my mother taught me was from Surah As -Saff:

"Nasrum min Allahi, wa fat'hun khareeb."

"Help from Allah and victory is near." (Surah As Saff 61:13)

I do not know whether I clung to these prayers out of desperation for my inadequacies or to give me hope. But either way, they had a profound effect on the outcome of my endeavors. Not only was I able to overcome my disability, but doors of opportunity started to open up that I never could have anticipated. I began to realize that my achievements went clearly above and beyond my effort.

After high school, I imagined that I would become an engineer. My father had different ideas and convinced me to pursue medicine. Perhaps he saw something in me that I never knew. As a result, I enjoyed unparalleled success in the field of medicine that no one who knew me could have ever anticipated. During my career I was able to publish over three hundred scientific articles and enjoy a worldwide reputation for bringing innovative advances to my discipline. I was cited by my peers to be one of the best cancer specialists in the United States.

During my fairy tale life and career, my relationship to Allah continued to get stronger. With every award, every promotion, and every discovery, it was becoming increasingly apparent to me that Allah was the master planner. It was He who was orchestrating my success and it is to Him that all credit is due. Over the course of my life, my reliance on Allah's help deepened. Similarly, the Quran continued to grow as a source of strength, peace, and comfort for me. My salah became more meaningful. Even the very first Surah (Fatiha), grew in meaning. The common refrain, "You only do we worship and You only do we seek help from," took on greater significance. But none of this would be possible, had I not been given the opportunity to reflect on my short-comings and come to rely on Allah throughout my life.

That "a-ha" moment of self-realization comes to each of us at different moments in our life. It may be difficult for the well-provided person to ever come to this but for those that face hardships, disability, or loss, the opportunities for self-assessment begin early. History is replete with example after example of orphans who have had to turn to Allah early in life. Once people recognize their inadequacy and turn to God, they achieve singular levels of success. On the contrary, those that never come to this realization (or quickly forget it) come to believe that they are the cause of their own success. These individuals eventually end up with disastrous outcomes.

Beyond the example of the Prophet, Islamic history has the stories of Imam Abu Hanifa, Imam Malik, Imam Shafi and many others who were orphaned early in life and turned to Allah for help. Not surprisingly, they too have become shining stars of the human race. The Quran is also filled with stories of the people of remembrance and those who bury the truth (kufr). Following these examples, Allah asks in the Quran, "Do you not see?" or "Do you not understand?" How do we answer that question? How many examples do we need?

This is a critical element of true success, and so it is a parent's utmost responsibility to teach their young adult children to reflect on who they are and how they view their relationship to Allah. Help always comes from Allah in good times and bad. The Prophet said, "Contemplating deeply for one hour (with sincerity) is better than 70 years of (mechanical) worship."

2. Knowledge

Adult education is also about the acquisition of knowledge. Early adulthood is not just a period of physical growth, but cognitive development. This is not limited to storing more facts, but learning what to do with the data, namely reason and analysis. The Quran pays particular emphasis on this aspect of our capabilities with over eight hundred verses asking us to go out and seek knowledge. In fact, the very first revelation of the Quran emphasizes the need for man to read and write.

"Read! In the name of your Lord who created.
Created man from a clinging substance.
Read, and your Lord is the most Generous —
Who taught by the pen,
Taught man that which he knew not." *(Surah Alaq 96: 1–5)*

Reading and writing is a fundamental pre-requisite to developing healthy self-awareness. By tapping into the wisdoms of past generations, we can live a more complete life in the present while also bequeathing a powerful legacy for the future. There is a very wise saying that says "there is no greater fool than an ignorant fool." Just as reading and writing is critical to understand who we are, it is equally, if not more necessary to understand who God is. Suffice it to say the very first commandment was, "Read!"

The Prophet (pbuh) underscored this commitment to knowledge when he said, "The acquisition of knowledge is compulsory for every Muslim, whether male or female." He also emphasized gaining knowledge does not stop with a university degree, but is a continuous process throughout a person's entire life. He said, "seek knowledge from the cradle to the grave."

Knowledge comes in different shapes and forms. There is the

knowledge you obtain from schooling, the professional knowledge that allows you to earn a living, and the knowledge of the Quran and Sunnah that can be obtained by reading and listening to presentations. But mere reading and listening are not a substitute for personal reflection, nor will they alone help you come to understand the essential meaning of the Quran. One must also actively sort through his own lived experience to uncover the gems of experiential knowledge that help solidify their understandings. As I have outlined in my own example, while experiential knowledge is not structured, it is in some ways the most important part of one's education, providing some of the deepest and most compelling insights into one's relationship with his Creator. Personal reflection is often the difference between understanding the Quran and Sunnah as abstract texts versus knowing Islam as a deeply personal lived experience.

"Are those who have knowledge and those who have no knowledge alike? Only the men of understanding are mindful."
(Surah Az Zumar, 39:9)

While Allah clearly makes a distinction between people of knowledge and those without it, He is not talking in terms of quantity but in terms of understanding. Memorizing the sports statistics could also be considered knowledge, but this knowledge alone does not make you a star player. That being said, a star player can use this knowledge to make himself a better player. So it is with knowledge of Allah. While we could spend an entire lifetime learning and memorizing all the books on Islam, we must remember that facts alone do not build a relationship with Allah. Relationships are developed through lived experience. Book knowledge can add to that, but not substitute for it.

So what then is useful knowledge? Some knowledge comes to us through Allah's revelations in the Quran. Unfortunately, the Quran can be a challenging book to understand if read like any ordinary book. The Quran can best be understood if one first understands the context of events in which Allah sent down His revelations. This begins to have added meaning when the context is superimposed on one's own life. If nothing else, this is the message of the Prophet's life.

Knowledge is key to developing faith. At many places throughout the Quran, Allah provides an explanation or narrates a historical event then poses the question "do you not understand?" (Surah Al An'am 6:32). In addition, Allah specifies that those who believe in Him, ask to be increased in knowledge:

"My Lord! Enrich me with knowledge." (Surah Ta'Ha, 20:114)

This is the perfect "dua," as it is only through knowledge that we can really know Allah. In the words of the Prophet (pbuh), "the best form of worship is the pursuit of knowledge," and "Contemplating deeply for one hour (with sincerity) is better than 70 years of (mechanical) worship."

3. "Tazkiah" (purification)

Prophet Abraham (pbuh) made the famous dua:

"Our Lord! send amongst them a Messenger of their own who shall rehearse Thy Signs to them and instruct them in Scripture and Wisdom, and purify them; for You are the Exalted in Might, the Wise." (Surah Al Baqarah, 2:129)

And Allah fulfilled His promise to Abraham (pbuh):

"A similar (favor have you already received) in that We have sent among you a Messenger of your own rehearsing to you Our signs,

and purifying you, and instructing you in Scripture and wisdom, and in new Knowledge." (Surah Al Baqarah, 2:151)

What does the Quran mean by purifying yourself? Allah swears by his creations and commands us as follows:

"And by the sun and its brightness;
And by the moon as it follows it (the sun)
And by the day as it shows up (the sun's) brightness;
And by the night as it conceals it (the sun);
And by the Heavens and He who built it;
And by the Earth and Him who spread it;
And by the Soul, He who proportioned it;

Then He showed him what is wrong for him and right for him; Indeed he succeeds who purifies his own self (i.e. obeys and performs all that Allah ordered, by following the true Faith of Islamic Monotheism and by doing righteous good deeds).

And indeed he fails who corrupts his own self."
(Surah As-Shams, 91:1-10)

This surah spells out the key to ultimate success: self-purification. Unfortunately arrogance prevents most people from taking this course. Just like the people of 'Ad and Thamud, man often deems himself the ultimate authority in deciding what is right and what is wrong, clearly defying what Allah has already made clear through his prophets. If only man realized who he is in relation to the universe!

While we believe that the Earth is over four billion years old, man's lifespan averages a measly 70+ years. He occupies the tiniest of space on Earth, yet he thinks he knows more about right and wrong than the one who created the "Heavens and the Earth and all that is therein." This kind of arrogance is blinding, and as Allah says in the Quran, the ultimate roadblock to achieving success.

Success requires purification. Purification requires constant introspection. Where am I now? How am I doing? Can I be better? What are my weaknesses? Am I being honest with myself? How about now? etc. This tireless process is the path of the righteous (saliheen), and it comes with Allah's promise of success. Self-purification comes from establishing the right balance in the relationship between oneself and Allah, and then adopting a lifestyle that manifests this balance. The best example of this is the life of the Prophet (pbuh). For that reason, we see that Allah reminds us to find success not just by obeying Allah, but by also following his messenger (pbuh).

Purification requires one to cling to those deeds that are pleasing to Allah and avoiding all evil. It is the thankfulness for all the miracles that surround us. It is in the redemption of mistakes that one inevitably makes in life either of omission or commission. Purification finally comes down to a genuine love for Allah and the Prophet (pbuh). Tazkiah is to surrender our lives to Allah and His messenger such that our actions are dictated by what might be most pleasing to Allah and His Messenger.

Therefore, actions such as inappropriate speech, racism, bigotry, greed, anger, jealousy, hatred and other vices that are abhorrent to Allah must be avoided at all cost. Actions that reflect the attributes of Allah as embodied by His several names are to be emulated. Mercy, kindness, charity, gratitude, honesty, trust and similar characteristics are the hallmarks of a pure heart. The developmental period of early adult life is the time to adopt and own these attributes while facing the challenges of this world.

12 | THE ROLE OF MUSLIM WOMEN

The best of women are those that find their happiness within their homes.

The latter part of the twentieth century has seen a great change in the role of women at home and in society. Surveys from 1976 show that most women considered getting married and having children as their first priority. Decades later that has been replaced with achieving professional success. As a result, the number of women who have remained unmarried has doubled from 8% in 1960 to 17% in 2012 and is continuing to rise. At the same time 41% of first-time marriages in the US end in divorce, with two-third of these initiated by the wife. While there are a number of reasons for this high divorce rate, there is no question that changing gender roles and increased opportunities for financial security have contributed to this problem. Muslim families are not immune to this trend. This pattern is now influencing the social and family structure of Muslim families as well. Sadly, this trend is such a departure from the role of women in Islam.

It is one of the unfortunate facts of history that both men and women have forgotten what a woman truly is. The Biblical story of Eve being created from Adam's rib has engendered a secondary role for women in the hierarchy of the human race. Throughout history there has existed a dichotomy in the way women have been perceived. On the one hand, women have been elevated to the Godhead and venerated in many religions and cultures across the world (Aphrodite among the Romans, Venus and Diana among the Greeks, Isis in Egypt, and the Mother Earth in Hindu mythology, Al-Uzza and Al-Lat among the pagan Arabs, and Mary as the mother of God, among Catholics). On the other hand, nearly all societies have had a patriarchal system of family life with women sometimes being treated no better than slaves or property.

In reality women have had little to no rights nor say in their lives. Women could not own property or run a business (with the exception of some elites), and were financially dependent on their male relatives--a father, husband, brother, etc. Daughters were sold in marriages for political or financial gain, and even to this day, are often considered a drain on family resources. In the days before Islam, newborn girls used to be buried alive. Today they are aborted or avoided altogether through in vitro selection. It is no wonder that women have risen up to demand their rights in human society.

During WWII, the demand for labor outstripped the supply of manpower. This allowed women to enter the workforce in large numbers and opened the door to a new sense of independence. While women have viewed this change as a liberating opportunity, they have exchanged one form of servitude for another. In reality women's lives have always been about work. In underdeveloped countries, women walk miles to gather wood and fetch water for the families. They are the ones who go to the market to buy essential goods, cook for and feed their families, clean their homes, and wash the clothes. While modern society has replaced many of these physical duties with automated machines that can do much of the hard labor, someone has to pay for the upfront and maintenance costs. Women have replaced the effort they spent on the upkeep of their homes by joining the workforce outside to bring in the cash to support the machines they now have to buy. Has replacing the master at home by the master at work been a fair exchange? Most women would say yes as this has given them a level of financial independence, confidence, and control of their own lives. This in many ways has been a good and positive change as it has diminished, but not eliminated, the abuse women were routinely subjected to. But there is abuse outside the home that cannot be ignored—women get paid less than men for the same amount of work. While this disparity certainly needs to be redressed, it has also created a creeping change in the psyche of women that men and women should be equal in all rights and functions of human endeavor, especially in family life and in the home.

How has this change affected Muslim women? By and large, educated Muslim women have bought into the idea of complete equality (which is different than equity) of the sexes. To be sure, in less educated circles, the patriarchal system still dominates. This whole idea of equality of the sexes has created a great deal of tension, conflict, and misunderstanding in many marriages. On this topic, the Quran states:

"Women have rights similar to those of men equitably, although men have a degree of responsibility above them. And Allah is Almighty, All-Wise." (Surah Al Baqarah 2:228)

Allah has made clear that the rights of women are similar but not the same as the rights of men. Furthermore, men have been charged with a greater responsibility not only to protect the rights of women, but to make sure both parties fulfill their responsibilities. Thus women who demand absolute equality are going against the dictates of Allah, and lack of understanding of womanhood itself.

Allah has bestowed special gifts on His creation differently. He imbued women with great psychological power when compared to men and to this day women continue to enjoy this superiority. This power is intrinsic, intuitive and subtle and women exercise this power in every relationship without even realizing what they do. There are many

books written on the subject of the differences and similarities between men and women. Most of them, such as "Men are from Mars and
women are from Venus" deal with the different ways men and women
react to different situations in their interpersonal relationships, but few
deal with the intrinsic psychological advantage women have. In nature,
females often make the decision of mate selection. They instinctively
base their decision on the future likelihood of survival of their offspring. Likewise, women are much more discriminating (where they
have a choice) of who they will marry. Men are far less discriminatory
and are more likely to be attracted purely by physical appearances.
Women invariably look to marry into higher social strata for economic
stability and security, while men are most likely to base their decision
on emotion rather than logic.

It is true that some women marry because they fall in love. There is
invariably a transactional element even in this relationship wherein the
woman requires to be wooed thus establishing a level of control over
the relationship. The process of courtship is nothing more than trans-
ferring control in a relationship. There is fundamentally nothing wrong
in this per se, but it highlights the psychological difference between
men and women. Most women do not even realize this game of psychological dominance that is so natural and intrinsic to their personality. A
quote from the Readers Digest of yesteryear says, "Women marry the
best man they can find and spend the rest of their lives changing him."
This psychological advantage that women have can be used to great
advantage in any relationship or can be very destructive. Many empires
have been won and lost on the actions of women. "Behind every great
man is a woman," is a popular saying that attests to the silent power
women wield. With such power already in their grasp, why do women
want to be equal to men? It is understandable that they should be paid
equal wages for equal work, but when they extend this to encroach
upon men's roles and responsibilities, we see a disruption of the balance Allah has created between the sexes. When Allah speaks of "men,
being responsible for women," he is clearly indicating that men need to
be aware of the psychological disparity and pitfalls they may encounter
and therefore it is their responsibility to be assertive in guarding the

family unit from internal and external manipulation and set the agenda and goals for the family.

The role of the Muslim woman is first and foremost to provide a safe, peaceful environment for the family unit. While the role of the husband is to provide for the physical well being and protection from external forces, the women is responsible for the psychological and mental well being of the family. Women are not required to do physical labor in support of the family; this is the husband's responsibility. The Quran says, "men are the protectors and maintainers of women." Any physical housework that a woman does is a form of "sadaqa" which Allah blesses with enormous rewards. However, if this is at the expense of family harmony, or if it causes mental anguish to family members, much of the rewards will get washed away. This is where Allah tests women's psychological superiority. If their efforts are in the best interest of the family, great success can be achieved. If, however, women choose to use their advantage selfishly by pursuing their own agenda, it can inflict great harm on the family.

The most important role for the Muslim woman is the role of the mother. For a very long time, women have been seen as nothing more than breeding factories. In past agrarian societies, having more children meant having more field hands. Given higher mortality rates, having more children was also insurance against calamities. But the real role of a mother is not just to bear children, but guide their development into strong Muslims.

The famous hadith narrated by Abu Hurairah, that is quoted frequently by everybody is when a man asked the Prophet (pbuh) "Who is most deserving of my good company?" The Prophet said, "Your mother." The man asked, "Then who?" The Prophet said "Your mother." The man asked again, "Then who?" The Prophet said, "Your mother." Only when asked a fourth time, did he reply "your Father."

Many of us fail to understand the full significance that the Prophet (pbuh) gave to mothers. (Remember he grew up without a mother himself). I believe the reason he mentioned the mother three times is because of the significant role she plays in the child's life. These three areas are as follows:

1. Gestation

2. Infancy and Childhood

3. Adolescence

1. Gestation

The very first reference to the mother is the fact that it was your mother's womb where your physical being was created and where you were nurtured and protected till you were ready to enter the world. In Arabic the mother's womb is actually called "rahma." Pregnancy is a very special event in the life of the woman. The child in her womb is an "amana"—a gift and a trust from Allah. How the woman deals with this trust very much determines the character and fate of the child in the future. Apart from the usual process of caring for the health of the fetus, such as good personal hygiene, nutrition, exercise and avoiding intoxicants, there is a lot more that a woman needs to focus on.

One of the most essential elements to early human development is the emotional equanimity of the mother. Depression, over excitement, anger, loud noises, and family conflicts can have a serious deleterious effect on fetal development and continue after the child is born. It has been shown that the mother's voice itself has a soothing effect on the fetus, as does soft harmonious music. This encourages early brain development in the fetus and facilitates neuronal connections in the brain. For Muslim women the lilting music of Quranic recitation should be a required part of prenatal activity especially if this is in the mother's own voice.

The second element is for the mother to think long and hard about the kind of individual she hopes her child will become in later life. She should focus on making extensive "dua" to Allah of her dreams for the future of the child. Most people say that they will be satisfied as long as the baby has five fingers and five toes. This is a demeaning way to look at Allah's gift. Instead one should pray that their child will become the best of human beings, a leader of the Muslim umma, and always remain under the protection of Allah's mercy and blessings. After all, Allah will listen to your prayers, but only if done with sincerity and pure intention. A mother should make a contract with Allah that she will do everything she can to provide the kind of childhood that will help her child become a strong and pious adult. No wonder the Prophet (pbuh) put the "mother" at the top of his list. The Quran says:

"We have commanded people to honor their parents. Their mothers bore them in hardship and delivered them in hardship. Their period of bearing and weaning is thirty months. In time, when the child reaches their prime at the age of forty, they pray, 'My Lord! Inspire me to always be thankful for Your favors which You blessed me and my parents with, and to do good deeds that please You. And instill righteousness in my offspring. I truly repent to You, and I truly submit to Your Will.'" (Surah Al Ahqaf 46:15)

When the mother fulfills her role, it becomes a debt that a child owes to his mother, not just for the hardships she bore in carrying him in her womb for nine months, but the blessings Allah has showered on him as a result of his mother's duas. While Allah asks us to honor both parents, he singles out mothers because of the debt that we can never repay them.

2. Infancy and Childhood

The second mention of mothers in the hadith is regarding the mother's role in shaping the personality of the child into a model as desired by Allah and established by the example of the Prophet (pbuh) and his companions. This is a mother's most important role. While there is no physical umbilical cord attaching the infant to the mother, there is an invisible cord that remains for years to come. During this period, the child is a lump of clay and the mother has the task of shaping and polishing the child into the most perfect specimen of a human being. While people like to talk about the difficulties of pregnancy and childbirth, this period of care is infinitely harder and requires a whole set of new skills.

A well-known Jewish proverb says, "God could not be everywhere so He created mothers." There are many cultures that recognize the importance of this role. The "Jewish mother" is famously recognized as the archetypical example of how parenting influences the success of their children, but this is not the only example. Those that watch the National Spelling Bee and similar competitions will see Hindu mothers as the driving force in their children's achievements. Unfortunately, this has not been a cultural strength of Muslim mothers. Quantity over quality has been the usual practice with only a modicum of attention to personality development. Instead, this task is left largely to "tawakkul" – a reliance on Allah, as long as the basic needs of the child are met. Muslim women need to recognize that there is no greater purpose to their lives than the "amana" Allah has entrusted them with in the care of their children. If a mother is entrusted with a million dollars, would she just leave it around, citing tawakkul? No, she would safeguard it and discharge her responsibilities as required of the trust. Is a child not worth more than a million dollars? Why then are we so cavalier with their upbringing? Yet many modern women would rather spend more and more time outside the home than in the home even with young children.

Even spending time at the masjid is given priority over young children. This is not religion. This is the opposite, because it is an abandonment of responsibility. Spending time with children requires a great deal of patience, understanding, love, and devotion. While love may come naturally, the other aspects of childrearing require a woman to put her child's needs ahead of her own.

A mother has to develop a new mindset that creates a harmonious, safe environment within the family that is without egos. A mother has to set an example of speech and behavior that the child will copy. The child has to see honesty in order to grow up to be honest. The child has to see kindness to grow up to be kind. A mother will be the child's teacher for the rest of his life. Children's problem solving and socio-emotional skills are largely learned from the mother. The love a mother pours into her child is largely responsible for the development of righteousness and morality. Certainly, all of this is a big task, but so is the title of "mother."

3. Adolescence

My mother was my teacher. She was the one who taught me the basics of Islam. She was the one who woke me every morning for fajr with the announcement "Assalattu khairum minun naum"--prayer is better than sleep. She taught me how to perform "wudu," and she was the one who read me stories of the Prophet (pbuh) and the companions (sometimes with tears streaming down her face). She told us about the heroes of Islam, of the great scientists and their discoveries, and she was the one who made great preparations during Eid and other key dates on the Islamic calendar. She made sure we all experienced Islam in the most positive way. Many times she would sit up with us while we prepared for exams. In the morning we read Surah Yasin together before leaving the house. At the door she would wave to us with a dua "Nasrum minal lahi wa fat'hun kharib"--When Allah's help is with you, victory is near. When we returned, she would make sure that there was something special to eat. Rarely would she ask about the test. Instead she would assure us that Allah knows what is best for us as long as we did not let Him down. That is a Muslim mother.

For all of these reasons, the Prophet (pbuh) elevated the status of women so highly. Why do Muslim women not realize the tremendous gift that Allah has given them? Why do they trade all the treasures of Allah's opportunities and blessings, just to be like men in worldly affairs?

Clearly the roles and rights of the mother and father are different. The father is no less important in a child's character and development. He has the responsibility to provide for the family and spends much of his time outside the house. In a child's early formative years he has much less opportunity to spend time with the children. Nonetheless, a child learns from interpersonal interactions within the family, especially how his father treats his wife and his mother.

The Prophet said, "the best of men are those who are best to their wives." I learned lessons watching my father interacting with the world outside. Though my father occupied an administrative position in government, the family was financially constrained. I witnessed many occasions when bribes were offered to him for favorable decisions, but my father was resolute in rejecting any such offers. His principled character made a profound impression on my young mind. I also saw how this translated into the high regard and admiration others had of him--his superiors, his colleagues, and his subordinates. As far as I am concerned this was worth many more millions than the bribes themselves. Watching my father, I learned that it is not what a father says that matters but what he does that is important for the child's learning and growth.

Finally, a woman's role as a wife is just as important. The home is the woman's castle and she is the master of it. As I have outlined above, she is responsible for the harmony and the smooth functioning of the home. While she is the master of the home she also serves it. It is her responsibility to make sure every member of the household is taken care of before her own needs. If she puts herself before the others, the family unit breaks down. Strife, conflict, and disorder folllow. The wife is fundamental to the husband's achievement in life. If the wife is primarily driven by the desire for a big house, a fancy car, jewelry, clothes, and appearances, then husbands must engage in the never-ending consumer rat race to satisfy the woman's desires. However, if the woman desires excellence in front of Allah (through character), then there is no limit to the heights a husband can achieve! If we need to look for a role model, there is no one better than Hadrat Khadija the wife of the

Prophet (pbuh). She was the richest businesswoman in Mecca but after her marriage she dedicated herself to supporting the Prophet (pbuh). Imagine if she had not supported the Prophet (pbuh) at the time of the very first revelation. Would the Prophet's (pbuh) mission have taken a different direction? Believing in her husband and abandoning her past religious and cultural traditions without a second thought she became the first convert to Islam and then was the most active recruiter of supporters from her immediate family to the Prophet's (pbuh) mission. There can be no better example of the role of a woman in Islam than her dedication to her husband and family.

13 | THE ROLE OF MUSLIM MEN

The best of men are those who are best to their families.

The role of men in Islam is pivotal to the health and vitality of the Muslim community. Allah has entrusted men with great responsibility from the beginning of creation. Allah blessed Adam with knowledge far beyond all of other creation. When He sent Adam to Earth as his viceroy (2:30), Allah laid down his expectations of Adam's role and gave him a purpose for his life on Earth. All men today are the inheritors of the charge Allah entrusted to Adam. In this capacity each one of us has to seriously consider our life's purpose and how we go about fulfilling our destiny.

There are seven distinct areas of responsibility that men have to undertake:

1. Righteousness in personal living

2. Raising righteous children

3. Harmony in family life

4. Honesty in business and work

5.   Caring for your neighbors

6.   Building a legacy of knowledge and charity

7.   Gratitude to Allah for the trust He placed in you

1. Righteousness in personal life

What does it mean to be righteous? Allah has defined righteousness in several ways in the Quran but the simplest definition, which He has emphasized repeatedly, is "to do good" in this world. When He states that He has created us as His viceroy, he is clearly stating that our role is as His employees. In the Quran He says:

"Indeed, Allah has purchased from the believers their lives and their properties [in exchange] for that they will have Paradise. They fight in the cause of Allah, so they kill and are killed. [It is] a true promise [binding] upon Him in the Torah and the Gospel and the Quran. And who is truer to his covenant than Allah? So rejoice in your transaction which you have contracted. And it is that which is the great attainment." (Surah At Tauba 9:111)

What else is our role as employees but to follow the instructions and perform the tasks Allah has asked of us. In the Quran, we read the stories of the prophets to understand clear examples of the task before us and to remind us how easy it is for us to stray from Allah's guidance. The stories also emphasize that the path we must take may not be easy. There will be distractions and allurements, and it will require a great deal of commitment, patience, and perseverance to achieve success. After giving us the stories of the prophets, Allah then placed before us the most complete picture of success, through tribulations and success, in the life of Prophet Muhammad (pbuh). To follow in the Prophets footsteps is therefore, the definition of righteousness.

Amongst the many virtues we can see in the Prophet, the element that stands out most was his caring and compassion for others. Allah emphasizes this to a great degree in the Quran:

"Righteousness is not that you turn your faces toward the east or the west, but [true] righteousness is [in] one who believes in Allah, the Last Day, the angels, the Book, and the prophets and gives wealth, in spite of love for it, to relatives, orphans, the needy, the traveler, those who ask [for help], and for freeing slaves; [and who] establishes prayer and gives zakah; [those who] fulfill their promise when they promise; and [those who] are patient in poverty and hardship and during battle. Those are the ones who have been true, and it is those who are the righteous." (Surah Al Baqarah 2:177)

True righteousness, therefore, starts first from taking care of those who are closest to you—your parents and your family—and then expand in concentric circles to your relatives, your neighbors, your community, your city, and then beyond to the rest of the world. Many are misled by focusing on the outside world first while neglecting the people in their home, often to be seen as pious by others. This is false piety. Caring should start early in life with care of your parents and siblings. Do not wait for your parents to grow old, when you think they will need you. Rather be the shoulder they lean on when they are young and still taking care of you. As much as the Prophet's grandfather, Abdul Muttalib, his uncle, Abu Talib, and Abu Talib's wife, Fatima, took care of the Prophet when he was young, the Prophet returned their love many times over. He served them in herding their camels and doing everything he could to support them. This is charity of the highest order! So do not wait for your loved ones to get old, because it may be too late and you will have lost the greatest opportunity to give the best of charity.

Various attributes of Islam, as highlighted by Allah in the Quran, have been emphasized by the companions of the Prophet. Hadrat Ali said, "Has not Allah Almighty sufficed you in His book wherein He said, 'Verily, Allah commands justice and excellence?' (16:90). Justice is to have a sense of fairness and excellence is to prefer others to yourself. What remains of manhood after this?"

Caliph Omar ibn Khattab said, "The foundation of a man is his intellect, his honor is in his religion, and his manhood is in his character."

The companion Hassan al-Basri commented that the entire religion of Islam is the embodiment of manhood. A Muslim man is not given honor because of his superior strength, loudness of his voice, domineering personality, or the ability to incite fear in others. Rather honor comes from his trustworthiness and his capacity to protect others by word and action. Controlling one's anger and the ability to forgive are integral parts of the manly ideal.

"Show forgiveness, enjoin good, and turn away from the ignorant."
(Surah Al A'raf 7:199)

A Muslim man understands that he is the servant of Allah carrying out the mission entrusted to him. He is not the master of anyone else nor is he answerable to another human for his actions. He lives to seek the pleasure of Allah and that is all that matters to him. Unfortunately, there are no half measures. You cannot be a little of this and a little of that. That is where many men make a mistake and think that they can overcome their character flaws by the volume of their ritual worship. Unfortunately, none of the rituals count for much if your actions have not been in keeping with the principles of Islam.

2. Raising righteous children

Young boys are greatly influenced by their mothers who are responsible for their direct sustenance and survival. But as they grow, boys subconsciously begin absorbing a tremendous number of cues from their father. In a normal household, he perceives his father as the protector and provider for the family. If his father is fulfilling his role, the boy invariably patterns his own behavior and mannerisms after his father. In history, many of the most successful men refer to their fathers as their most important role model in their lives.

In early childhood the father is often a boy's playmate. This is the perfect time to teach the child about critical building blocks of character. Winning and losing, sharing, generosity, kindness, language, and many more traits are passed down and are most impactful in play rather than in lectures and punishments. The father's most important role is to imbue in the boy a sense of security and love. The boy grows to recognize that his father is the "safe harbor" of his life and this feeling will remain with him throughout his entire life. It is for this reason that he has to see his father exhibiting the best of human qualities—gentleness, humor, equality, fairness, honesty, and most of all trustworthiness. As the child grows, the relation changes gradually from a playmate to a teacher. The child actively learns skills such as the maintenance of the home. He gets help with homework and school projects, and most importantly receives an education in the Quran and Sunnah. By this I do not mean simply teaching the child to read the Quran, but actually getting him to understand the Quran's purpose and message. Essential teaching tools such as bedtime stories of the prophets and Sahabah, Islamic games, and watching videos together can enhance the value of such topics in a child's mind. In addition, discussion of such topics as peer pressure influences, sex education, sports and politics should be encouraged.

As the child turns to his adolescent years the role of the father will change again. They may spend less time together, but now the father acts more as a friend maintaining the "safe harbor" relationship for the child. Nothing the child says should be dismissed as nonsense, but should be discussed openly without being judgmental. Furthermore, the child should be exposed to as wide a circle of relatives as possible. He should be encouraged to broaden his worldview especially if some of the relatives are less fortunate in worldly position. He should be able to learn from his father's example in how to love and care for other family members.

Remember that a righteous child is the greatest legacy a father can leave behind. It is a blessing that he can actually take with him to the Hereafter.

3. Harmony in family life

Early adulthood is a critical period of a man's life. This is the time when he makes one of the most important decisions that will affect the rest of his life. This decision revolves around the question of who to marry and start a family. Many men fall into this situation without much thought to the consequences of their decision. Some get married due to family pressure, some get married because it is the expected thing to do, and some simply fall in love. In arranged marriages, the process of choosing a spouse is heavily influenced by elders who often rely on pedigree, status, wealth, and looks. Often what follows is a persuasion campaign that results in a marriage where there may be little compatibility. Historically these marriages lasted because of some of the same pressures that resulted in the union in the first place and for the welfare of the children--these are marriages of tolerance. It is not to say that some arranged marriages are not highly successful, but they tend to be few and far between.

The second type of marriages are "relational" marriages. In these, the partners get to know each other and may even fall in love. The vast majority of these are based on short term emotional responses like physical attraction, likes and dislikes, and occasionally common endeavors like jobs, sports, or other hobbies. It is assumed that life will sort itself out as time goes on. In reality, as time passes life gets messier while the initial excitement and perceived compatibility has long faded.

How should a Muslim man approach this important crossroad?

First, he must establish his own goals. By now we have made it clear that his goal should be to "become the best human possible in the service of Allah." To this end, he needs to find a partner that shares this goal. When he is looking for a partner, the criteria he should be looking for is humility, kindness, humor, and generosity of spirit. Like men, women who are confidant in who they are, are not dependent on external validation. These women are rare but worth the effort to find. Intelligent women recognize that happiness is an internal state of mind. But most women never recognize this truth and enter a marriage expecting their husbands to make them happy by catering to their whims and desires.

Women often ask, "Do you love me?" They are often seeking approval and asking to be placed on a pedestal. Feeding this inadequacy is a sure way to lose your way in life. In most every relationship, the best way to identify these individuals is to see how much attention they need from their spouses. Therefore, the way to approach this pitfall is to be honest and upfront about your goals and game plan in life. Be upfront and tell them that you are passionate about the Prophet (pbuh) and your goal is to follow in his footsteps by serving humanity. Tell them that you are looking for a partner, who can, not only help achieve these results, but surpass them. Do not worry if many prospective partners do not share your vision. After all, you have to sift through a lot of stones before you find a gem.

Does this mean you should plan to spend much of your time at the masjid? Far from it, for it is not rituals alone that are important. Rather you should enjoy the many gifts Allah has bestowed on and around you with a partner who also finds fulfillment in the simpler things of life. You should strive to have a family that values each member and helps each other to achieve their highest potential as a human being who finds happiness in serving the community for the pleasure of Allah.

A real marriage is like a melding of two bodies, heart and soul. Each is an extension of the other not unlike your hands and your feet. We protect our hands and feet because they can bring us great blessings and happiness. Similarly, we should protect and care for our spouses who bring us far more. If you would not abuse your hands and feet why would you abuse or try to dominate your spouse? Like our limbs, our spouses work best when they work with us, and us with them. The Prophet (pbuh) said, "the best of men are those that are best to their families, and I am the best to my family."

Finally, it should be added that the best wives are those whose husbands are happy. It has been narrated on the authority of Umm Salama (ra) that Rasul'Allah (pbuh) said: "If a woman dies in a state when her husband is pleased with her, she will enter Paradise." (Tirmidhi)

Another hadith narrated by Abu Hurayrah reported that Allah's Messenger (pbuh) said: "When a woman prays her five (prayers), fasts her month (Ramadan), preserves her chastity, and obeys her husband, she will be told (on the Day of Judgment), "Enter Jannah from any of its (eight) gates."

Every act that a wife performs for her husband is sadaqah, just as the sadaqah a husband gives when he looks kindly on his wife. Imagine how special it is that perhaps the easiest path to paradise may be for the husband and wife to work for each other's mutual happiness!

It is also important to remember that marriage is a social contract in Islam that is bound by legal rules that are especially important in cases of divorce or death. These rules are supposed to be codified in a contract between both parties at the time of the marriage ceremony. However, present-day family law in the West does not often follow nor respect traditional contracts. Many times, these contracts are in Urdu, Arabic, or other languages that neither the groom nor bride can read. They only understand that there is an agreed on mehr (dowry), which is the least of what the contract specifies. Most importantly, there are also no Islamic courts that can enforce the rest of the contract, which makes them meaningless. In the West, the only rule for marriage is to say, "I do," in front of a Justice of the Peace. This has led to a number of abuses and court fights in cases of disagreement. It is therefore important to return to the Islamic concept of a clearly crafted marriage contract that both parties find equitable and agree on before the marriage itself. While some in the West may call this a "prenuptial agreement" (which has its negative connotations), Islam requires this to protect the rights of both parties and especially the welfare of children. That such a contract is not currently in general use is a major flaw in our society and should become customary in any future marriage. If you cannot agree on a contract before marriage, what are the chances you will live in peace and harmony afterwards?

4. Honesty in business and work

Developing professional expertise is a necessary part of life. The process starts early with formal education, schooling, and often college. As a Muslim it is imperative to strive for excellence. Seeking knowledge is considered as important as time spent in prayer. A Muslim should approach his chosen profession as service to Allah and not as a means to garner wealth or power.

Few people realize how Allah's rewards come to us when our efforts are purposefully redirected. In my own life this realization came to me in the middle of my career as a cancer physician. One morning I had just seen an important patient who I had successfully treated for pancreatic cancer. He was the brother of the University president and had initially presented with a form of the cancer with a very low survival rate (<5yrs). But many years later, here was my patient who not only had survived five years, but was thriving. I was so elated that I felt like I was walking on air the rest of the day.

Later that same day, (on the recommendation of the University president) the Chairman of the Board of the University asked me to see his eighty-year old mother who was scheduled to undergo surgery the next day for a small skin cancer on her eyelid. After examining her, I recommended that I could easily get rid of this cancer with treatment rather than surgery that could disfigure her eyelid. The cure rate for this cancer with radiation was 99.999%. I was told to go ahead and I started treatments for her. At the end of treatment, the cancer was still there when it should have disappeared well before!

This memory reminds me of the Muslim experience at the Battle of Hunayn. The Muslims for the first time had an army of thousands and thought their numbers were sufficient to overcome the enemy. However, they were ambushed and nearly annihilated. They only barely won the day when the Prophet (pbuh) rallied the Muslim forces to victory. Unlike many of the overconfident Muslims, the Prophet (pbuh) never attempted anything without first putting his trust in Allah.

After the experience seeing both patients, I prayed for forgiveness and asked for Allah's help in the future. Three weeks later when the elderly patient returned, the cancer was gone without leaving a single blemish. Ever since that day, I vowed to first ask Allah for help, and then use my knowledge to do the most good that I can. Since then I have enjoyed a great career with national and international accolade, all due to Allah's special blessings alone.

What I have also learned is that a job is not just a means to a paycheck. A job is where you constantly apply your knowledge to improve outcomes by constantly asking the question, how can I do the job a little better? To improve you may have to seek new knowledge, learn new skills, test different strategies and martial a variety of your God given talents. If you ask for Allah's help in this endeavor you will find ideas flow to you in a surprisingly easy manner. This is what has enabled me to write over 300 scientific articles in my career. None of it would have been possible if Allah had not given me the inspiration and guidance. One of the few things we take into the afterlife are the blessings for leaving new knowledge that has benefited humanity. Do not be satisfied with the status quo, rather constantly ask the question "Why?" Recall the story of Abraham (pbuh). His father was a rich idol maker and Abraham (pbuh) could have been satisfied with a comfortable life, except that he kept asking the question 'why" until he found the final answer. In our professions, we too need to pursue this same sense of inquiry and urgency.

A final element of professional life is honesty. First and foremost, we need to be honest with ourselves and acknowledge what is due to us and what is due to Allah. Secondly, we need to project the best aqlaaq and adl in our dealing with others. We should not aim for success by bringing others down (i.e. backbiting and creating mischief). The result will be far from success of any kind. Rather, we should represent the very best of Islam in our work and our treatment of our colleagues.

5. Care of your neighbors

It has been well established that Islam is a communal religion. It is the well being of the community rather than the individual that matters. The community includes your immediate family and your close relatives, parents, siblings, aunts, uncles, and cousins. Secondarily your community includes your friends and your immediate neighbors. When the Quran and Sunnah talks of your neighbors, the impression is that it is only the people who live next to you. In fact, the people closely related to you are your primary neighbors. The care and the rights of these relatives is a primary responsibility for us. Ibn Abbas reported: The Prophet, peace and blessings be upon him, said, "He is not a believer whose stomach is filled while the neighbor to his side goes hungry." It is therefore essential to look beyond your immediate household to make sure your parents and siblings are well cared for.

There are a number of hadith that also refer to your next door neighbors as well. The Prophet (pbuh) said, "By Allah, he is not a believer! By Allah, he is not a believer! By Allah, he is not a believer." It was asked, "Who is that, O Messenger of Allah?" He said, "One whose neighbor does not feel safe from his evil" (Sahih Bukhari).

On another occasion the Prophet (pbuh) referred us to the example of a women who prayed, gave charity, and fasted a great deal, but also harmed her neighbors with her speech (by insulting them). About her, he said, "She will go to hell." A man said: "O messenger of Allah! There is (another) woman who is well-known for how little she fasts and prays, but she gives charity from the dried yogurt she makes and she does not harm her neighbors." He said, "She will go to paradise." These and other hadith underline the value of having excellent character and deep compassion for those around us.

6. Building a legacy of knowledge and charity

In previous chapters we have discussed the importance of acquiring knowledge and building a legacy. Those who can, should transmit their knowledge freely to others. The Prophet (pbuh) said "The best of charity is when a Muslim man gains knowledge, then he teaches it to his Muslim brother." In the modern age, information is such a vital source of power that it has essentially replaced military might as a determinant of a superior civilization. Muslims need to regain their rightful place as leaders amongst men. We must ask Allah to increase us in knowledge, just as Moses did (Surah TaHa, 25-28), and then strive to reach the top. In another Hadith the Prophet said, "Whoever takes a path upon which to obtain knowledge, Allah makes the path to Paradise easy for him." May Allah give us the wisdom to recognize this vital element of being a Muslim man and help us achieve success.

6. Gratitude to Allah for the trust He placed in you

Finally, we must always keep in mind that we are Allah's creation. Nothing happens except that it is according to His Will. This includes how He created us and endowed unique gifts to each and everyone of us. The Quran says this very clearly "For should you try to count Allah's blessings, you could never compute them" (An-Nahl 16:19). Reflecting on Surah Rehman (55) will only add to this feeling of immense awe and gratitude. As Allah details all of his gifts to us He asks, "Now which of the blessings of your Lord will you deny?"

Certainly, one of the best forms of prayer is expressing frequent gratitude to Allah for the gifts he has already bestowed upon us. Unfortunately, many of us waste our time because we are too concerned with what we don't have. We put our wants and desires ahead of what Allah deems suitable for us. This is a prescription for disaster. Just look around and you will find that we are surrounded by miracle after miracle that keeps us safe from harm and provides good health and sustenance. Should we not then be thankful?

But gratitude cannot be in words alone. It requires action. Take the example of the Prophet (pbuh). The person most dear to him was his wife Khadija. Hadrat Khadija was the greatest example of a complete Muslim role model. She devoted her life to the service of her husband. She gave him six children and when the first revelation came, she was the first to accept Islam and support the Prophet even when the Prophet (pbuh) himself was not sure of his mission. She was the one who brought in her sisters and nephews into Islam as among the first to support the Prophet (pbuh). During the ban years (Quran Years 7-9), she stood by the Prophet (pbuh) and suffered enormous deprivation, existing on grasses and bark of trees for food. This deprivation eventually took her life in QY 10. The Prophet (pbuh) was devastated and the memory of this moment never left him. Nonetheless, after the conquest of Mecca, the Prophet (pbuh) forgave the very people who had caused the death of his beloved wife. This is gratitude to Allah in action.

On another occasion in Medina, the Prophet (pbuh) saw a man pass by and said aloud that that man is destined for Jannah. The same thing happened over the next few days and the sahaba wondered what was so special about this person that he was promised Jannah. A few of them decided to follow him around. They found him to be just a common hard-working man. They couldn't identify anything that seemed unusually special in his daily routine. They finally decided to ask him about it and the man replied that before he sleeps each night he makes sure to forgive any and all those who might have wronged him that day. And for this act alone, the Prophet (pbuh) had singled him out as a person of Jannah. Forgiving others is a true sign of gratitude for it counterbalances all the blessings we receive each day that we never stop to think about.

In summary the seven roles a Muslim man has to fulfill are as follows:

1. Righteousness in personal living – be a good man

2. Raising righteous children - be a devoted father

3.   Harmony in family life - be a caring husband

4.   Honesty in business and work - be a strong leader

5.   Care of your neighbors - be a sensitive neighbor

6.   Building a legacy of knowledge-be an inspiring teacher

7.   Gratitude to Allah - be a true servant of Allah

14 | LEGACY

Your character is the best legacy you can leave in this world.

What is the value of a life that is well lived? The world often measures your worth by weight of the fortunes you leave behind. But for Muslims this is not a measure of success, but rather a sign of failure. We come into this world with nothing and we leave just as we arrived. Yet in our actions and deeds we can create a legacy that we can simultaneously leave behind and take with us to the Hereafter. Unfortunately, many people begin to start thinking of their legacy towards the latter part of their lives, when (if they are even so blessed) they only have a few years left. So how and when should we start preparing for our legacy?

The word "Sawab" is often used to imply a reward that Allah bestows on you for doing something good. The word "Azaab" is used to denote the opposite. Unfortunately, people live their entire lives calculating their sawab and azaab, as if they were balancing a checkbook hoping to come out on top. We need to think differently about these terms. Few single events exist in isolation. Almost every action is like casting a stone in a pond. Where the stone lands, there is a splash, followed by ripples. The splash you create, is the "Sawab" or "Azaab" you get credited with. The ripples you created whether intentional or otherwise is the legacy you create from your action. The bigger the stone, the bigger will be the legacy. In the Quran there is a commandment to fulfill your required ibaadat (Salat and Sawm) but there is equal, if not more, emphasis on performing good deeds. Each ibaadat will get you one "sawab," but every good deed gets you the benefit both of the "sawab" and the ripples that it creates which is the legacy. That is why, for example, a Hadith of the Prophet (pbuh) says "to visit a sick person is better than seventy years of prayer."

Muslims today have prioritized personal prayer, fasting, Hajj, and Umrah rather than the accumulated deeds that create a beneficial legacy in this world and which we can carry with us to the next. After all, which is better: to perform ten pilgrimages or to invest that same money into feeding the hungry, caring for refugees, or creating employment for the needy?

Building a legacy should start from a very young age. After all, children are the legacy of their parents. Teaching them aqlaaq (good behavior and character) will not only start the process of building their legacy, but build yours as well. They are the ripples of your pond, just as we can be the ripples of Prophet Muhammad's legacy (pbuh), and he is part of the ripple initiated by Prophet Abraham's (pbuh) before him.

What are good deeds? Good deeds begin with thinking well of others, avoiding racial and other prejudices, having empathy for those who are suffering and less fortunate, and fighting against those who oppress any of God's creation. Good deeds start from your tongue: a smile, a greeting, a kind word, soft voice, avoidance of harsh or foul language, praise, etc. Good deeds mean lending a helping hand. It may be as simple as helping a family member, a colleague, or a stranger in distress. None of these actions require you to be rich. They are simple acts that can be a part of everyday life from the youngest to the oldest.

Beyond these simple daily actions, good deeds include the sharing of knowledge (learned or discovered) that benefits humanity. Educating others creates a ripple effect that brings one of the highest rewards. For example, a student of yours may take what he learned and use it to make huge discoveries that may change the face of humanity.

Finally, good deeds include sharing one's wealth. While many people see this as giving charity, it's important to always remember that your possessions do not actually belong to you, but are a gift from Allah for you to use and enjoy. While, you cannot give what is not yours to begin with, you can certainly share it with others. This is again a fundamental Islamic principle that needs to be instilled in children at an early stage. The Arabic word "Sadaqah" has wrongly been translated as "voluntary charity," when in fact it should be translated as "righteousness." The "Siddique" is one who is righteous.

This famous Hadith of the Prophet (pbuh) says "When a man dies, his deeds come to an end, except for three: except for a continuous charity, knowledge by which people derive benefit, and a pious son who prays for him."

Much of this hadith is self-explanatory except that no one knows the time of his death. The Quran speaks to this: "For all people a term has been set: and when [the end of] their term approaches, they can neither delay it by a single moment, nor can they advance it." (Surah Al A'raf, 7:34). Hence the time to prepare your legacy is now, rather than wait for old age, which may never come. The hadith also points to the best form of sadaqah, which is "continuous." A classic example can be seen from the life of Hadrat Uthman. When Muslims in Medina were thirsty for water, he did not just give them a specified amount to drink. Rather, he bought the "well of Rumah" at Medina so the Muslims could have all the water they wanted. His legacy encompasses everyone who has drunk from that well from that time until today. This is inline with the common saying: "Give a man a fish and you feed him for a day; teach a man to fish and you feed him for a lifetime."

Following the example of Hadrat Uthman, we therefore need to invest in institution building (such as building educational programs and vocational training) rather than limiting ourselves to relief work alone.

But this kind of effort requires a thoughtful communal leadership, otherwise individuals will pursue their fragmentary efforts.

The second element of the Hadith is the emphasis on knowledge. When Allah created Adam, the first thing He did was to teach him the names of things. This knowledge established the superiority of man over all other beings. The ability to learn and use language differentiates man over the rest of creation. Over millennia, each generation of humans has added another layer of understanding to what was passed on to them. As a result, humans now live in markedly improved living conditions over previous generations. Each discovery creates a long-lasting ripple effect. No doubt Muslims should lead this race to benefit humanity. Even the simplest transfer of knowledge from teaching someone to read and write, to teaching someone an understanding of the Quran can have significant down-stream effects.

On the subject of acquiring knowledge the Prophet said:

"Seeking knowledge is a (religious) duty on every Muslim."

"Seeking knowledge for one hour is better than praying for seventy years."

"It is better to teach knowledge one hour in the night than to pray all night."

These statements convey not only the immediate benefits of seeking knowledge, but the rewards of creating an ongoing legacy. Every man and woman should ask, "What knowledge am I leaving behind for future generations?" The answer will show us how we have been investing our time, and whether we have missed valuable opportunities.

The final element of this trifecta is to bring up pious children. Just as we are the legacy of our parents, so will our children be ours. Honoring ancestors is a tradition of every ancient civilization. Whereas many of these civilizations developed rituals and traditions to honor their ancestors, in Islam, the only way to honor them is to live a life that conforms to the Quran and Sunnah. Piety is not in the rituals but in the purity of our hearts and in the goodness of our deeds. If you take the time to raise children properly, every good deed they perform, becomes part of your legacy.

Many of us who are fortunate to know of the political and social achievements of our ancestors may feel a sense of pride in our ancestry, even thinking that this is our legacy. This is not our legacy but our heritage. Just as we are their legacy, our legacy comes from our present and future conduct. The sooner we recognize this, the sooner we can take advantage of all the opportunities that come our way. In summary start young and do not stop!

15 | ARROGANCE (KIBR)

Arrogance is the greatest of all sins.

In the Judeo-Christian tradition, Adam's disobedience to God is often referred to as the "original sin." In stark contrast, Islam teaches us that God had prepared Adam for this challenge in order to teach him the first principles of right and wrong (obedience and disobedience). Allah was preparing Adam to be his representative on earth. We see in the Quran that when Adam realized his mistake, he immediately repented and asked for forgiveness. Allah was so pleased with him that He forgave Adam and gifted him with revelation, so as to secure him and his progeny from all fear and grief.

In stark contrast to Adam's humility before Allah, we have the story of Iblees. When Allah asked the angels to bow down to Adam, Iblees refused. Unlike Adam's momentary lapse, Iblees's disobedience was fueled by a deep-seated belief that he was superior to man.

"And behold, We said to the angels: 'Bow down to Adam,' and they bowed down. Not so Iblis: he refused and was haughty: He was of those who reject Faith." (Surah Al Baqarah 2:34)

Allah's reaction to Iblees's disobedience was severe--he was banished from Allah's presence forever. This unprecedented sin (the arrogance/disobedience cycle) is the deadliest of all forms of disobedience and should be considered the real **"Original Sin."**

While Christianity has absolved man from the sin of arrogance by shifting all the blame to Adam, the Quran is very explicit that arrogance and pride are the single most abhorrent traits for which there is no salvation.

"[To them] it will be said, 'Enter the gates of Hell to abide eternally therein, and wretched is the residence of the arrogant.'"
(Surah Az Zumar 39:72)

Many of us do not think we are arrogant because we may not strut about wearing silk gowns and fine feathers. But the truth is, arrogance can be very sneaky—it creeps into your heart when your connection to Allah weakens. How many of us are proud of who we are or what we are or what we have achieved in this world? Perhaps we call this pride, but pride is the first sneaky step to the path of arrogance. The truth is that every blessing we receive from Allah is a moment when we can slip up. We feel pride in all sorts of things such as our ancestry, our status, our looks, our wealth, our children, our home, our cars, and sometimes even our pets. Does any of this really belong to us? Each of these are gifts from Allah and should have the opposite effect of eliciting gratitude and humility. But instead we are often and easily seduced by the idea of bringing about our own success. A vicious cycle emerges when the more Allah gives someone, the more he look down on others who were not given a similar gift. Pride has quickly transformed into arrogance, and arrogance fuels disobedience.

"And do not turn your face away from people in contempt, nor go about in the land exulting overmuch; surely Allah does not love any self-conceited boaster." (Surah Luqman 31:18)

Being wary of pride does not mean that we should not enjoy Allah's blessings, for that would be ingratitude. Rather we should enjoy these blessings as long as we give credit to Allah and share our good fortune with others. If you are successful at work, help others succeed. If you have wealth, share with others who are in need. In personal matters like your looks and talents, enjoy the gifts Allah has given you but avoid strutting around seeking the praise of others. The more we are given, the more we have to share to keep pride from entering our psyche. **We are not better than others in what we have, but in what we give,** for as the Prophet (pbuh) said in his last sermon, "None is better than another but by good deeds." The Quran too places great emphasis on this point:

"Indeed, the most noble of you in the sight of Allah is the most righ-teous of you." (Surah Al Hujurat 49 :13)

It has been my lifelong observation that few people realize life is a circle. Have you heard the expression, "what goes around, comes around?" Many times I have observed that Allah often tests us with the things we are most proud of. As a physician, I have seen many patients who were proud of their looks suffer from facial or head and neck can-cers. I have seen vain women lose their lush hair as a result of disease or treatment. Proud parents who live vicariously through the success of their children later are abandoned in old age by those very same children. Boasting rich people are very often brought low by financial disasters. In my own case, I was very proud of my memory. I easily memorized huge volumes of anatomy and physiology in my early years, but now I have difficulty memorizing two lines of the Quran.

In the Quran we find example after example of how Allah punished the arrogant throughout history. In Surah Al Kahf, we see the story of the two gardeners--the one who was arrogant saw his garden destroyed in the blink of an eye. In Surah TaHa, Allah describes the miserable fate of Pharaoh who arrogantly rejected Allah's messenger, even after being delivered from calamity after calamity. In Surah Lahab, we see the fate of the Prophet's (pbuh) own uncle, who was unmatched in his arrogance towards the Prophet and his message:

"May the hands of Abu Lahab perish, may he (himself) perish.
His wealth avails him not, neither what he had earned.
Soon will he roast in a flaming fire,
And his wife, the bearer of the firewood,
Upon her neck a rope of twisted palm–fiber."
(Surah Lahab 111)

Think also when Allah asked for a sacrifice from Cain and Abel, the sons of Adam. Cain kept the very best animals as his own. Allah therefore rejected his offering. In contrast, Prophet Abraham (pbuh) was willing to sacrifice his beloved son who was born miraculously in Abraham's old age without a second thought. Allah spared this son and then He rewarded him by making him the father of mighty nations. The take-home message here, is that we may be tested by having to share our most beloved gifts. It is a test of attachment, and those who remain attached to Allah, ultimately succeed.

After Allah has made his message clear to us, the most serious form of arrogance is the rejection of Allah, His angels, His prophets, His books, the Last Day, and His divine Decree. Allah says in the Quran:

"Verily! Those who disdain My worship (because of arrogance),
they will surely enter Hell in humiliation!"
(Surah Al Mu'min, 40:60)

I believe that Muslim efforts to convert people to Islam should not focus so much on the practice of religion but really the acceptance of

Allah as their one and only master. The practice of religion will come easily only after this connection is firmly established and Allah's help will make every hardship easy.

"You alone we worship and you alone we ask for help."
(Surah Al Fatiha 1:5)

One unique area where arrogance can specifically creep in is among those who have acquired knowledge in religious matters. It is easy to fall into the trap that we know better than others about what is right and wrong. In fact, Imam Al-Ghazali stated, "People of knowledge are in greater danger of arrogance than anyone else," because they may look down on others who are less learned than themselves. Sharing knowledge and teaching others is a must for all Muslims, but no one should assume that they know everything there is to know. This is especially true for people who study the religious texts but do not live by those words (thereby showing that they do not understand them). The Quran likens these scholars to donkeys carrying religious books on their backs (Surah Al Jumuah 62:5) and says that they are "wretched." **The true measure of wisdom is not how much knowledge we carry in our heads (or on our backs), but how humbled we have become by the weight of understanding them and then living out those principles sincerely in daily practice.**

How do we avoid pride and arrogance? It is quite simple. If you are a billionaire, live like a millionaire; if you are a millionaire, live like a commoner; and if you are a commoner, live like a faqir. Unfortunately, the world teaches us to follow the opposite course. But the world is not our master. As we learn in the Quran, all power belongs only to Allah alone--He is the One we should serve.

All sins are forgivable sins of man except for the sin of arrogance. **Arrogance is the "sin of Satan."** Satan thought he was better than Adam for a contrived reason (fire is better than clay) and using this fact, he thought he knew better than God by not bowing down.

This is the source of his shirk (disbelief). In that moment, Satan worshipped his own whim over God's Decree. He preferred his own will over His Will. Arrogance is "THE SIN" that Allah does not forgive. It is the root sin to every spiritual disease. Always remember that **"Iblees is arrogance, and arrogance is Iblees"** so don't sell your soul like Iblees for the paltry rewards of this world. Every other slip-up can be washed away when we repent sincerely and ask for His mercy.

It is narrated on the authority of 'Abdullah bin Mas'ud that the Prophet (pbuh) said, "none shall enter the Fire (of Hell) who has in his heart the weight of a mustard seed of Imaan and none shall enter Paradise who has in his heart the weight of a mustard seed of pride." What use is all of our worship if we present ourselves before Allah carrying a mountain of pride and arrogance when a mere mustard seed's worth is enough to negate all the good that we did in this life?

16 | RACISM

Racism is abhorrent to Allah and the Prophet (pbuh) – avoid it at all cost.

Towards the end of the sixth century, at the time of the birth of the Prophet Muhammad (pbuh), the city of Mecca was a major economic and political hub. People came from all parts of Arabia and Africa to perform the pilgrimage and honor the many idols housed at the Kaaba. Mecca was also an important waypoint along the North-South trading route connecting the rich valleys of Yemen to the splendors of the Byzantine Empire in Syria. From the West, Abyssinian traders and merchants also arrived from across the Red Sea. Not surprisingly, Mecca witnessed an extensive mingling of races, cultures and ideas. There was also a flourishing slave trade with many Meccans owning and trading slaves. As with most places around the world, Meccan culture developed a tribal hierarchy of haves and have-nots. Those with wealth became the elites and leaders, while those with limited resources became the poor underbelly of society. This led not only to individual elitism but also to tribal elitism. Wealth led to elitism. Elitism led to arrogance. And arrogance led to racism (looking down on others because of their color, creed, economic status, tribal affiliation, disabilities, etc.)

From the beginning, the Prophet (pbuh) recognized the widespread unfairness and abuse that was prevalent in Meccan society. He became increasingly distressed at the Zulm (oppression) of the weaker elements of society. It was soon after the first revelation of the Quran (610 AD) that he was tasked by Allah to fight the root cause of human arrogance that not only pervaded his society, but infects the world at large. This was a herculean task that had been given to most every prophet and had been met with some success and a lot of failures.

History shows us the Prophet (pbuh) successfully achieved the task that was placed upon him. He achieved this, not by lofty lectures and flourishing admonishments, but by his singular example, which was guided by the Quran.

Very early in his mission, few of the Prophet's family and friends accepted his message. Instead the Prophet (pbuh) faced constant abuse and rejection. Ironically, his nastiest critics recognized the miraculous beauty of the Quran. They knew that the Prophet (pbuh) was unlettered (could not read or write) and had never composed a poem in his forty years of life. Surely the passages must come from someone special. Yet these critics were not willing to accept that these words were the words of the Almighty (Allah).

Walid ibn Mughirah was the chief of the most powerful and wealthy tribe in Mecca, Bani Maqzum. Though a fierce critic of the Prophet, the words of the Quran had made a significant impression upon him. Walid came to the Prophet's (pbuh) uncle and guardian, Abu Talib, and indicated that he and his friends were willing to listen to Muhammad (pbuh) but on the condition that they not have to sit with the freed black slaves that were always around the Prophet (pbuh). Abu Talib was excited with their request and presented this proposal to the Prophet (pbuh). Perhaps a meeting like this could provide a tremendous breakthrough for the Prophet to help get his message to Mecca's most elite circles. If Bani Maqzum supported the Prophet, they could help amplify the Prophet's message among the rest of the Arabs. Even other companions of the Prophet were excited by this opportunity. But Allah sent these three verses of Surah Al An'am:

"And turn not away those who invoke their Lord, morning and afternoon seeking His Face. You are accountable for them in nothing, and they are accountable for you in nothing, that you may turn them away, and thus become of the Zalimun (unjust)." (Surah Al An'am 6:52)

Hearing these revelations, the Prophet (pbuh) immediately rejected such an offer, even though such a refusal would cause greater opposition to his message and oppression of the nascent Muslim community.

Unfortunately, this episode is not well known amongst most lay Muslims. It is a powerful statement of the integrity of Islam and a true reflection of Allah's message that all men are created equal and that Allah makes no difference between individuals on the basis of color, wealth, or social status.

"Oh men! Behold, We have created you all out of a male and a female, and have made you into nations and tribes, so that you might come to know one another. Verily, the noblest of you in the sight of Allah is the one who is most deeply conscious of Him. Behold, Allah is All-Knowing, All-Aware." (Surah Al Hujurat 49:13).

All that counts is what is in the heart of a person with respect to his Creator. There are only two types of individuals before Allah: those that love Him, and those that reject Him. In the example cited above, we see that one who truly loves Allah will never compromise basic Islamic principles (no matter how inconvenient) such as racial equality and justice. We see this in the famous quote of the Prophet, who, when offered material wealth if he stopped preaching, answered, "By Allah, if they put the sun in my right hand and the moon in my left, I would not abandon it."

Human equality is a cardinal tenet of Islamic faith and cannot be compromised for any reason. That Allah has created many of us in different molds is one of his miracles indeed and He says this clearly in the Quran:

"And among His wonders is the creation of the heavens and the earth, and the diversity of your tongues and colors. For in this, behold, there are messages indeed for all who are possessed of innate knowledge!" (Surah Ar Rum 30:22).

During the life of the Prophet (pbuh) there were many examples wherein he made it quite clear to the companions that Allah severely frowns upon racism and reserves very harsh punishment for it. One such example occurred in Medina when Bilal ibn Rabbah (ra) was accosted by a highly regarded sahaba, Abu Darda (ra), for repayment of a loan that was past due. Abu Darda (ra) addressed Bilal (ra) as "you son of a black woman..."

The Prophet (pbuh) overheard the remark and rebuked Abu Darda (ra) "Have you reproached Bilal about his mother? By the one who revealed the Book to Muhammad, none is more virtuous over another except by righteous deeds. You have none but an insignificant amount."

Abu Darda (ra) was so shaken by this, he immediately fell down at the feet of Bilal (ra) asking for forgiveness. As was the greatness of Bilal (ra), he immediately picked Abu Darda up and hugged him.

Today derogatory names are attached to all types of people on the basis of color, ethnicity, nationality, tribal affiliations, social status and more. These terms are so commonly used, it is easy to start using them oneself, which is why it is imperative to teach our children otherwise. Allah is severe with those who look down on others. All the good we do in this world will not save us if we do not cleanse our hearts of this sin.

Another powerful episode comes after the conquest of Mecca. At the time of Asr on the very first day, the Prophet (pbuh) asked Bilal (ra) to climb to the top of the Kaaba and call out the "Azaan" in front of the whole Qureysh. On hearing the Azaan being called by a former slave, some Meccans remarked, "it is good that my father has died before being witness to such an event or he would have died seeing this!" Another person remarked "could not they find anyone better than this black crow?"

In response, Allah immediately sent down angel Gabriel with newly revealed verses from Surah Hujarath:

"O you who have believed, let not a people ridicule [another] people; perhaps they may be better than them; nor let women ridicule [other] women; perhaps they may be better than them. And do not insult one another and do not call each other by [offensive] nicknames. Wretched is the name of disobedience after [one's] faith. And whoever does not repent – then it is those who are the wrongdoers." *(Surah Hujarath 49:52)*

Allah has made it very clear that racism is abhorrent to Him and is cause for severe punishment. The only distinction Allah has made amongst people is based on their faith. The words of the Prophet's (pbuh) final sermon should leave an indelible mark in every Muslim's mind.

"O people, your Lord is one and your father Adam is one. There is no virtue of an Arab over a foreigner nor a foreigner over an Arab, and neither white skin over black skin nor black skin over white skin, except by righteousness."

We all have been guilty at some point or other of knowingly or unknowingly acting prejudiced against others. The good news is that Allah has promised forgiveness for those who repent with sincerity. Like Abu Darda, we need to stay humble and reach out to those we may have disrespected.

17 | ZULM

All your good deeds will be for naught for one act of Zulm –
so beware.

The Prophet (pbuh) said in a famous Hadith (Qudsi) that "Allah Almighty said: O my servants, I have forbidden injustice for myself and I have forbidden it among you, so do not oppress one another." (Narrated by Abu Dhar Ghaffari)

The word "forbidden" is such an absolute term but has received short shrift in Islamic education and discourse. If one was to be asked what is Islam, one could easily describe it in three words: "the prohibition of injustice." We often talk about all the other prohibitions in Islam but rarely about this the most important of prohibitions. Why is this? Perhaps it is because injustice is so pervasive in society that it is largely accepted as the norm unless some catastrophic event such as overt genocide or enslavement bothers our conscience.

Is this what Allah was talking about when he made injustice haram for us? I do not think so, as this would be too obvious. Rather I believe the injustice Allah is talking about occurs in the everyday aspects of life. It is in the dealings within your family, at the supermarket, or at the masjid.

The golden rule of any and all religions is: "do unto others as you would have them do unto you." Rarely is this practiced. Lying and deceit are so commonplace that we separate them into small lies and big lies, thinking that it is only the big ones with overt consequences that are prohibited.

The Prophet (pbuh) said that "a miser can be a Muslim, a coward can be a Muslim but a liar can never be a Muslim." Why is there such an emphasis against lying? It is because lying is at the root of all injustice, and injustice is at the root of all Zulm. What is Zulm? The usual English translation is "oppression," generally taken as "oppression of others" but in reality Zulm has a much broader meaning. The actual meaning of Zulm is "darkness." The real oppression in Zulm is the oppression on oneself. No matter how much a human can oppress another, it pales in comparison to the oppression he does to himself.

There are a multitude of reasons why people lie. Most of the time it is either to protect oneself and others, or it is in an attempt to deceive others for profit or gain. Unfortunately like many other vices, lying is part of human nature. Children learn to lie at a very early age (2 + years). If the consequence of this lying is disregarded, the behavior becomes reinforced. Perhaps most destructive of all is when liars start believing their own lies. This leads to a state of self-deception that destroys all character. Once you reach this stage, it is impossible to recover any semblance of normal behavior.

Many of us justify small lies on the basis of not hurting others, such as when someone asks their spouse for feedback. But we should not ask for the advice of others if we are not open to hearing the truth.

It is reported by Abu Hurairah that the Prophet (pbuh) said, "Among the signs of a hypocrite are three, even if he fasts and prays and claims to be a Muslim, when he speaks he lies, when he gives a promise he breaks it, and when he is trusted he betrays."

The act of lying is a very dark sin. It is far more serious than other prohibitions that we take so seriously (such as eating pork, drinking, gambling, etc.). Deceiving another person has two components: the first is in the injury to the other person, and the second is in incurring the displeasure of Allah. Fortunately, Allah is All-Merciful and if you ask for His forgiveness He will forgive you. But the person you deceived may not forgive you, or may not even know to forgive you. Rather he will carry that debt of yours to the Hereafter and according to several narrations, will be repaid with the good deeds you thought were reserved for you. What a losing proposition! Muslims need to recognize the dangers of deceit and rise above it. When we wonder why Muslim countries are in the doldrums, we need not look beyond the level of lying and deception that is commonplace in those societies. Why would Allah help such people?

On almost every page of the Quran there is a reference to Zulm of one kind or another. The word Zulm has been specifically mentioned 20 times but alluded to in 120 verses. Derivatives of the root word have been alluded to 316 times in the Quran. Why then do we not pay more attention to this word, considering that many other frequently cited prohibitions are only mentioned a handful of times?

There are two types of Zulm that Allah considers most heinous. The oppressive ruler is the worst, and is one of the four categories of people Allah hates most. The second category of Zulm is religious oppression.

POLITICO-RELIGIOUS OPPRESSION

Since the beginning of time, human history has witnessed the suppression of religious practice by some over others. The first recorded case was when Cain murdered his brother Abel. Ironically, the underlying motivation for such oppression stems from forces outside of religion itself. In Cain's case, he was fueled by personal jealousy (because God did not accept his sacrificial offering).

In the modern era, the same scenario plays out on a larger scale. Religious practices of some are suppressed by others in the name of religion, but in reality, the oppression is motivated by some non-religious cause. In Nazi Germany, for example, the Jews proved a convenient scapegoat for the country's post WWI economic decline. As such, religious oppression is more commonly a tool of unscrupulous politicians who use the easily inflammable passions of an ignorant population to garner political leadership for themselves. These same politicians then exploit the very masses that they used to gain political power for their personal benefit. In describing these recurring, historical phenomena, Marx bluntly called religion the "opiate of the masses."

The result of such exploitation can be seen in the example of the Balkan experience in the 1990s. Though appealing to nationalistic and religious pride, the genocide of Muslims in Bosnia did little to improve the quality of life of the average Serb. In fact, the annual per capita income of the average Serb dropped from $6000 a year in 1991 to $ 1200 in 1999. Meanwhile, unlike the common populace, the political leadership in Serbia got stronger and richer, growing ever more arrogant. As for the oppressed, Bosnian and Kosovar, communities were devastated.

Every major religion espouses tolerance yet, often their religious leaders abuse their position for political or financial gain. Islam may be particularly vulnerable to this kind of abuse because the word "submission" is fundamental to the definition of Islam itself. However, this submission is to Allah alone and not to any mortal authority. Unfortunately, Muslims have often abdicated this authority to religious leaders. This pattern results in the grim history of sectarianism we see throughout Islamic history. Those who claim to know the Quran and hadith well should be aware of Allah's warning regarding Zulm.

"And those who work corruption in the earth, theirs shall be the curse, and theirs the Evil Abode." (Surah Ar–Ra'd 13:25)

This warning is not only for religious leaders, but for all of us to be wary of exceeding the boundaries that Allah has laid down for us. It is in our responsibilities to our families, friends and neighbors that humility, honesty and trustworthiness define every word we speak and every action we take. There is nothing that is hidden from Allah and so we have to ask ourselves: would we behave in an untoward or abusive manner before our bosses at work or in front of a judge? Why then should our behavior be any less in front of Allah? Deceit, lying, and abuse cannot be overcome by any number of prayers. We must look inward and change our state. Otherwise, we suffer the most from our blinded actions. Surah Fatir warns us of Zulm, saying "But of them are some who wrong themselves." (Surah Fatir 35:32)

18 | THE BIBLE AND THE QURAN

The Bible is a book created by men. The Quran is the first person word of Allah.

THE BIBLE

The Bible consists of the Old Testament which predates Christianity (also known as the Hebrew Bible) and the New Testament, which Christians claim contains the life and teachings of Jesus Christ. In mainstream Christian Bibles there are 66 books (39 from the Old Testament and 27 from the New Testament). While the Catholic Bible consists of 73 books and the Eastern Orthodox Church has 78 books, they both share the same 27 books of the New Testament.

Compilation:

The Old Testament was a compilation of manuscripts written over a millennium by over 40 different authors. During this nearly thousand-year period, the socio-political and economic circumstances of the Hebrews changed dramatically. These changes were also manifest in the Old Testament which likewise saw constant revision. The first five books are often attributed to Moses, but clearly Moses could not have written about his own death and burial while he lived.

The books of the Old Testament provide a history of the Jews, their basic creed of monotheism (belief in the One God), and the laws (613 commandments) that made up their side of their covenant with God. If they followed the book, God would favor them over all others. When one reads the Old Testament, it is clearly apparent that men (with or without divine inspiration), were the authors who chronicled the events and stories of the Hebrew prophets that were sent to the Jews. Why were men the authors and not God? Although there are passages that read, "God said to (so and so)..." there are also countless stories of rape, adultery, deceit, mayhem, and murder. For example we see that Joshua was commanded to kill all the men, woman, and children of Jericho (Joshua:8). Prophet David apparently committed adultery (Samuel 11: 2-5, Deuteronomy 2) and Prophet Noah could be found drunk and naked after the flood. And when Noah's son, Ham, revealed his nakedness to others, Noah cursed Ham's grandchildren (Genesis 9: 20-21). Clearly these deplorable stories reflect their human authors, not an Almighty God. That leaves us to ask: What else is fictitious in the Old Testament?

The Christian view of the Old Testament seems peculiar. On the one hand they accept these stories as part of their Bible, but then reject the very God depicted in the Old Testament as harsh, unyielding, and unloving. Moreover, they repudiate the divine laws God had laid down in the Old Testament and the notion that He directed the people to worship Him alone! For Christians, the special covenant between God and the Hebrews no longer applied to them. Ironically, they found it necessary to keep the Old Testament as part of their scripture, not to follow it (God forbid!), but to provide a shield of legitimacy to a fledgling religion that would come to be known as Christianity.

So did Jesus reject the Old Testament? We see that in fact, it was the exact opposite! Jesus was a practicing Jewish Rabbi who not only lived by the laws of the Old Testament, but strove to bring his people back from the corruption that had led so many Jews ignoring God's commands. Jesus makes a powerful statement to this effect:

"Do not think that I have come to abolish the Law or the Prophets; I have not come to abolish them but to fulfill them. For truly I tell you, until heaven and earth disappear, not the smallest letter, not the least stroke of a pen, will by any means disappear from the Law until everything is accomplished." (Matthew 5:17-18)

Jesus was circumcised as per Jewish law as were the people who followed him. His followers were also practicing Jews during his life and even after. So why have Christians discarded the fundamental teachings of Jesus? It would appear that after Jesus died, many interpretations were offered of what his ministry meant to different people in different parts of the world around Palestine. Many theologies evolved; some persisted but most perished. Perhaps the most influential of all was the Hellenistic influence a Greek Jew named Paul. His theology gained ascendency over all others, and subsequently redefined Christ's teachings into an all-together new religion, which has dominated until this day--"Pauline Christianity."

In sharp contrast to the above message of Jesus, Paul preached that, "Christ has abolished the law which was a wall of hostility." (Ephesians 2:15) Paul emphasized in thirty-six other letters in the Bible that the Laws of Moses no longer apply to Christians. Jesus by his own words came to reinforce the Law of Moses and Paul abrogated Jesus's primary message!! As a result modern Christianity in reality is Paulinism and not the religion of Jesus. **In a stunning admission of this fact the Catholic Church in an official capacity admitted in the New Jerome Biblical Commentary that the message and followers of Jesus died out soon after Jesus himself and were replaced by the theology of Paul, and they added that Jesus's religion was likely reborn in Arabia several centuries later as Islam.**

At first, this new religion had no textual scripture. There were, however, many stories of the last few years of Jesus's life that were circulating around. As centers of Christian worship required a better means of communication between the preachers of this new theology, various people started writing down some of the 2nd and 3rd hand stories they had heard about Jesus. While some of these stories were better received than others, four of them (written between 60 and 100 AD) were deemed to be most representative of Jesus' life. The four Gospels form the backbone of the new religion. These gospels are attributed to Mark (60 AD.), Mathew and Luke (both 70-80 AD), and John (90-100 AD). These four books form the bulk of the New Testament, which is followed by letters written by Paul (7) and then several epistles by other authors. Meanwhile, many other gospel manuscripts (at least 13 others that have been discovered) were discarded and burnt. Those that survived and/or have been discovered are referred to as the "Apocryphal" texts.

What then are the Gospels? They are biographies of the life of Jesus covering only a short period of his life. Are they then the word of God? Even if you believe Jesus was God, a major percentage of words attributed to Jesus are considered inauthentic (see the red-letter edition of the Bible). How can purported biographies of Jesus, as special as he was, be considered divine scripture? After all, a biography is just a story of a person's life. There are dozens of biographies of Thomas Jefferson, but none of them carry the weight of the US Constitution. Just as it would be foolish to consider Jefferson's life as the body of Laws to run a country, why is this approach taken with the New Testament?

Different biographers write from different perspectives depending on their socio-political leanings. No wonder there have been vast interpretive differences of events throughout history. So it is with the Gospels. What is even more troublesome of the Gospel stories is that they do not even tell the stories of Jesus in his own language: Aramaic. At best they are translated tales written in Greek, Syriac, and other languages, making them vulnerable to distortion with every hand-off. No wonder the four Gospels have such major differences with each other. The first three Gospels are supposedly built on the earliest work--the Gospel of Mark--and are thus called Synoptic Gospels because they seem to see eye-to-eye. And even then, these four books have marked differences.

The story and circumstances of Jesus' birth are radically different as are several events in his life (for a deep study, see Bart Ehrman's "Jesus interrupted"). Jesus' genealogy makes no sense in Mathew and Luke's Gospels especially if you consider Jesus' immaculate conception. And then again, if he was God how could he have a human genealogy? The stories of Jesus' death are even more divergent. His trial by Pilate, his crucifixion, his demeanor, his words all seem to be from different storytellers. Yet Christian theologians have been content massaging these divergent narratives into a new theology that cannot be supported from the written texts. But if the word is wrong, why call it the Gospel?

Jesus never claimed to be divine in the Gospels. He worshiped the God of Israel. Yet Christians made him divine by drawing oblique inferences from writings of people with socio-political agendas decades after his life. Much of this is attributed to Paul of Tarsus--a Jewish Pharisee, who never met Jesus but discovered a new theology based on a vision. Paul had to overcome a big hurdle in that Jesus's crucifixion, as a common criminal, was inconsistent with that of a Messiah of the Jews. He therefore created the redemption theology of the "Original Sin" based on the sacrifice of the "Son" of God. The "son" of God concept was common to many Greek, Egyptian and Persian (Mithraism) religions. In contrast, the Old Testament specifically denies a liability of sins being inherited by the offspring:

"The child will not share the guilt of the parent, nor will the parent share the guilt of the child. The righteousness of the righteous will be credited to them, and the wickedness of the wicked will be charged against them." (Ezekiel 18:19-20)

Christians got around this problem by rejecting the God of the Old Testament and His commandments, but nonetheless keeping the Old Testament in their liturgy to give pseudo-credibility to the fledgling religion. If not, the Pauline Christianity would have been rejected vehemently. Christianity survived by pretending it was a nuance of Judaic tradition and not an entirely new theology. Though it claims to be Abrahamic, there is not a single mention of Abraham in Christian worship or any of its beliefs. Although Jesus mentions Abraham as "our father" based on his Jewish identity, Paul's Christianity specifically targeted Gentiles, those specifically not from Abraham's progeny. Ironic that Christians would like to have it both ways in rejecting Abraham's religion yet claiming that their faith is also Abrahamic!

Certainly Abraham never ascribed to a triune God (Trinity). Christians refer to John's Gospel (5:7-8) as evidence of the Trinity, though it has been well established that this section is a spurious addition to the text that was added much later.

Another fundamental question for Christians is whether God died on the cross. How does God die? They also say that he was resurrected, which means he did not actually die. But if "God, the son" did not actually die, then where is the sacrifice? Why the charade? Additionally, Christians believe that on the Day of Judgment, Jesus will be sitting at the right hand of God. It defies logic that, if God the father, God the son, and the Holy Ghost are one and the same, God could be sitting on the right hand of God?

From an intellectual position, the Trinity is simply illogical. The gospels have some biographical value but as to theology, they are fundamentally incoherent and cannot be accepted as a basis for a world religion or the word of God.

THE QURAN

The Quran is distinct from every other book in the world. Unlike the Bible, it clearly has a single author, delivered in the voice of that author. It reads in the form of advice, warning, and instructions. Unlike the Bible, it is not a long sequential narration. Rather it was delivered in numerous separate installments over a period of twenty-three years. At the end of 23 years, it was divinely arranged together into a composite treatise which is the form we currently have today.

Who was the author of the Quran?

The Quran answers this question without any ambiguity. Its author is no less than the Creator of all the Worlds--everything in the Heavens and the Earth belong to Him. The author describes Himself, by saying that while His attributes are infinite, He can be best known through His divine attributes as laid out in the Quran such as Ar-Rahman and Ar-Raheem (The Most Merciful, the Entirely Mercy-giving). He lists ninety-nine attributes that describe His limitless power and glory. He also uses the name "Allah," which encompasses all of His attributes. Allah can be translated not just as God but as "All-Mighty God."

Who transmitted the Quran?

His name was Muhammad (pbuh), an orphan Arab child, born in Mecca to the tribe of Quraysh. Muhammad grew up in a society of idolatry and tribal conflicts (jahiliya). He was an unlettered (could not read or write) shepherd who grew up to become a merchant tradesman. Muhammad (pbuh) was very dissatisfied with Mecca's idolatry and culture of exploitation and injustice. He rejected the idols of Mecca and would often retire to a cave to meditate. At the age of forty he received a visitation by Angel Gabriel with a message from Allah:

"Read! In the name of your Lord, who has created (all that exists)
Has created man from a clot (a piece of thick coagulated blood)
Read! And your Lord is most generous,
Who taught (writing) by the pen,
Has taught man which he knew not." (Surah Alaq 96:1-5)

This was the first revelation of a sequence of narrations from Allah that lasted twenty-three years.

Why did it take twenty-three years to receive the revelations and not a single event?

Understanding the method of Quranic transmission is critical to appreciating what the Quran really is. It is not a novel nor a biography. As stated earlier, it is unlike anything that came before it or anything that has followed. The Quran is a book that uncovers the fundamental truths of human origin and the purpose of life. The Quran is a guidebook for mankind. It speaks to every soul who seeks to perfect his divine purpose, and in the process, take the quickest road back to his Lord.

The Quran's first task was to make Muhammad (pbuh) recognize he was chosen by Allah to be His messenger who would bring a message meant to transform a society gone wrong. Idolatry is the gravest sin to the one true God. Transforming this society would require a monumental effort at multiple levels: social, political, cultural, economic and religious. But first Muhammad (pbuh) had to be convinced of his mission. He had to understand the enormous task he was being asked to do.

It is understandable that he may have had misgivings. Perhaps he thought, "Why me? I can neither read nor write. I am an orphan from one of the poorer tribes with little or no leverage in society!" Thankfully the process of revelation and the support of his family made him realize that he had been entrusted with this ultimate challenge and that he had no choice but to undertake the mission with absolute commitment. The next installment of revelations started the process of preparing the Prophet for his task. Clearly the fundamental message was that he was to bring society back to the religion of their forefather, Abraham "the Hanif." The Quran warned him that like past prophets, his journey would be extremely difficult, often riddled with monumental challenges. As such, he was given the examples of the great prophets who had come before him. They too brought the same message from Allah. They too had experienced extreme rejection, ridicule and persecution. This was also going to be his fate as well. And like the earlier prophets, his success would depend on his ability to face these challenges with grace, kindness, and resolve.

As Allah warned, the first twelve years of the Prophet's mission often seemed insurmountable. But the Quran's timely revelations provided the Prophet and his small group of companions with the emotional and psychological support they needed. The verses are soothing and encouraging. They tell the listener not to lose heart but to remain firm in the face of adversity, for in the end, success will be theirs. As events eventually played out, Allah's promise attests to the truth of the Quran. Who else could predict that in a short period of twenty-three years, Mecca would become the center of the true Abrahamic faith (Milat-e-Ibrahim). Who else could predict that pagan Arabia would be completely transformed by the Prophet and his companions, ushering in a civilization unlike any in human history? Is this not miracle enough to attest to the truth of the Quran?

During the first twelve years, the Quran was helping the Prophet become a master craftsman. Far from his boyhood days as a shepherd, he was now being trained as a metaphorical blacksmith. How does one start in a new field? How do you set up a forge and use strange looking tools? Dumping a six-hundred page manual on him would not help him succeed. Rather, a step-by-step coaching process would allow him to build his forge, collect his scrap iron, put it through the fire, and mold it into the sharpest and finest steel. This was the Quranic process for the Prophet and his small group of companions. They were put through many fires: rejected by family, ostracized from society, and denied tribal protection. And while society provided the heat during the day, it was the coolness of the Quran at night that tempered iron into steel.

After twelve years, the Prophet (pbuh) and his companions were now ready for the next stage of their journey. The next ten years were about mass production. We see this shift in the Medinan surahs, because a proper factory requires rules and regulations to run safely and efficiently. Because the later fires were not as severe as the initial ones, it was easier for newcomers to follow the first Muslims. However, the danger of slippage was even greater, because these newcomers had not been tempered by the same heat as the earliest Muslims. The rules of society were now necessary and required, otherwise it would be easy come- easy go, as had happened to people who had followed earlier prophets. The revelations during the final ten years were a guidance to mankind on how to stay on the straight path and follow the religion of Abraham (Milat-e-Ibrahim) that was mandated by Allah. In no uncertain terms, it defines what is acceptable and unacceptable to Allah. It explains how we can best conduct our affairs within our family and within society.

The Quran therefore is a unique book: it is a process manual, it is a lesson in spiritual history of the world, it is an encyclopedia of the wonders of the universe, it is a source of knowledge from our Creator, and a source of knowledge about our Creator. The Quran not only explains the purpose of our creation, but also guides us to fulfill our greatest destiny.

How do we know that the Quran is truly divine revelation and not from Muhammad (pbuh)?

First and foremost, any student of the Quran can see that the Quran is instructing Muhammad (pbuh), coaching and supporting him through an entire twenty-three year journey. One cannot first build a computer to help write a manual to explain how to build a computer. So it was that the Quran was a manual instructing the Prophet on how to build an entirely new society. This guidance often came through stories of previous prophets, detailing their trials and tribulations. How could the prophet possibly have access to any of this information? Some of his contemporaries claimed that Muhammad (pbuh) could have learned these stories from Christians or Jews. But the truth is that most of these stories were unknown by any Arabs. There was no Arabic translation of the Bible at the time of Muhammad (pbuh). Furthermore, many of the Quranic stories contain far more detail than in previous texts. An example of differences is in the story of Jesus. In the Quran, he speaks as an infant to defend his mother against the charge of fornication. Although this story cannot be found in the Bible, a recent discovery in 1945 uncovered the same story in an ancient parchment among the Nag Hamadi scrolls. Similarly, the story of Jesus blowing life into clay pigeons is not in the Bible but again in the "Infancy Gospel of Thomas" discovered in 1945 AD. It should also be noted that compared to earlier scriptures, the Quran portrays each prophet as a model of excellence. This is in stark contrast to the Old and New Testament.

The proof of the Quran's authenticity can also be found in its scientific genius. The Quran contains a number of references to astronomical phenomena, especially the rotation of planets. This only came to human knowledge in the middle of the last century. In addition, we see astounding references to biological phenomenon such as embryology, animal husbandry, agricultural science, among others. It would be simply impossible for the Prophet to know any of these miracles of nature. While the Quran is not a book of history or science, Allah points out his miracles in the natural world so that we can understand His creation, and appreciate the harmony, functionality, and precision that goes into it. When we witness the wonder of creation, it points us back to the Creator.

Recent non-Muslims scholars have made a concerted effort to undermine the authenticity of the Quran by examining textual styles, arrangement of words, and the lack of a linear storyline (as found in the Bible). In contrast, the Quran's non-linear style attests to the magic of the Quran. The story of Moses appears in many separate chapters rather than a single narrative. Each segment of the story is apropos to the timeliness of the coaching given to the Prophet (pbuh) and his community. Yet despite all these various snippets, the entire narrative, when pieced together is completely coherent and without a single discrepancy. The same can be said for several other prophets. It is an unbelievable stretch of the imagination to think that an unlettered shepherd could conceivably bring together these piecemeal narratives over twenty-three years into a master copy. It would be difficult even with modern computers.

With regard to the language of the Quran, it is obvious to any reader that Allah uses a variety of textual arrangements to get His message across. Sometimes prose, sometimes poetry, the verses of the Quran hit the mark in every circumstance and every context. In fact, this was so unique to the Arabs, who prided themselves on the excellence of their language and poetry, that many were absolutely overwhelmed by the eloquence of the Quran. For many the language of the Quran is its single greatest proof.

How was the Quran compiled?

The Prophet would transmit the revelations he received to his companions who memorized them and wrote them down on animal skin parchments and/or bones of animals. Angel Gabriel is said to have reviewed the arrangement of the Quran in its entirety with the Prophet (pbuh) during the last Ramadan of his life. One of the great miracles of the Quran is that many companions had memorized the entire collection of verses (hifz) during the life of the Prophet (pbuh) just as many hundreds of thousands of people have ever since. After the Prophet's (pbuh) death the first Caliph (Abu Bakr) was advised that the community was losing many of the huffaz in various confrontations against the apostate tribes. In response, he commissioned the scribe of the Prophet, Zaid ibn Thabit, to assemble a complete copy of the Quran. This then was given to the second Caliph (Umar) at the death of Hadrat Abu Bakr.

To further crystalize the final assembly of the Quran, Hadrat Umar instituted the Taraweeh prayer during the month of Ramadan in which the whole Quran was sequentially recited in front of the entire Muslim congregation. This was led by one of the most learned men of the time, Ubay ibn K'ab. Some critics decry the oral transmission of spiritual texts given the chance for error. And while it is true that any spoken word can be changed from one mouth to the next, those who criticize the Quran on this have never been to a Taraweeh prayer. When an Imam who recites the Quran strays even in one letter of a single word, there are ten people who jump in to correct him. This eliminates any chance of deviant readings or inaccurate transmission of the text. On the contrary, it is a process of constant surveillance against forgery that continues to this very day, fourteen centuries later.

After the death of Hadrat Umar the original copy of the Quran was passed onto his daughter Hafsa, who also had been the Prophet's (pbuh) wife. During the time of the third Caliph (Uthman) more and more Muslims from different Arab lands entered Islam. With this came pronunciation differences due to regional differences in spoken Arabic. In an attempt to eliminate inauthentic variances, Hadrat Uthman commissioned Zaid ibn Thabit, the scribe of the Prophet (pbuh), to once again obtain the copy of the Quran from Hadrat Hafsa (which was in the textual language of the Quraysh) and make copies of it to be distributed to the various provinces. Meanwhile all variant copies were collected and destroyed. Hadrat Uthman himself was known to have memorized the entire Quran, which he would recite nightly. The Quran we have today (known as the Uthmani Mushaf) is the one that was assembled within the first year of the Prophet's (pbuh) death.

When scholars debate textual interpretations of the Quran they are often puzzled by statements and words that appear inexplicable to them. The Quran specifically states that there are many passages that remain beyond one's understanding (muthashabihat), and that we should avoid wasting time arguing over these. Rather we should concentrate on the verses that are clear and definitive (muhkamat). To be sure, the creed of Islam found in the Quran is clear and unambiguous.

Finally, modern detractors of the Quran should take note of a recent study conducted at the University of Birmingham in 2015, which analyzed a copy of the Quran known as the Sana Manuscript. It was discovered in 1972, and radio-carbon dated between the years 632- 671 AD with 99% accuracy.

That makes it one of the oldest known copies of the Quran written close to the time of Muhammad (pbuh). The findings in 2015 of the Birmingham Manuscripts lead Joseph E. B. Lumbard, Assistant Professor of Classical Islam, Brandeis University, to comment:

"These recent empirical findings are of fundamental importance. They establish that as regards the broad outlines of the history of the compilation and codification of the Quranic text, the classical Islamic sources are far more reliable than had hitherto been assumed. Such findings thus render the vast majority of Western revisionist theories regarding the historical origins of the Quran untenable."

19 | THE QURAN IN MECCA

The journey from Jahilliyah to Islam.

The Quran was revealed to Prophet Muhammad (pbuh) in small incremental passages over a twenty-three year period (610 to 633 AD) in Arabia, mostly in the cities of Mecca and Medina. The Prophet was 40 years old when he received the first revelation from the angel Gabriel during one of his meditative retreats in the cave of Hira, in the mountains above Mecca.

"Read! In the name of your Lord who created man, out of a (mere) clot of congealed blood." (Surah Al Alaq 96:1)

Mecca, at the time of the Prophet, was a center of great religious activity. At the center lay the Kaaba, surrounded by 365 idols. The vibrant religious tourism created a rich and prosperous society that became a trading hub between Syria and Yemen. Ironically the Kaaba had been built by Prophet Abraham and his son Ishmael as a house devoted to the worship of the Creator of the Heavens and the Earth, the "One true God." Over generations the people of Arabia had become polytheists worshiping the idols they created and housed in the Kaaba.

Prophet Muhammad (pbuh), although born in the family of the keepers of the Kaaba, had rejected the worship of the idols. Yet he was recognized as "Al Amin"- the truthful one, by his peers for his extraordinary moral conduct. During his thirties, the Prophet would withdraw to the cave of Hira to meditate, far away from the commotion in Mecca. When he received his first revelation, the shock of Gabriel's visitation nearly overwhelmed him. But after assurances from his wife Khadija and the Nestorian monk Waraqa, he came to accept that Gabriel's message was truly from God, and he was being tasked with a mission to bring the message of God, not only to the people of Mecca, but to spread it to the rest of the world.

For the next 12 years in Mecca the Prophet Muhammed (pbuh) received intermittent messages from God, who referred to Himself by many names, the chief of which was Allah- the one true God. Surprisingly, almost two-thirds of the Quran (81 of 114 Surahs) was revealed during this 12-year period. It is addressed to three main audiences: the Prophet Muhammad (pbuh), the believers, and the disbelievers.

The initial revelations revealed much of who Allah is, His many attributes, His purpose for the creation of mankind, and His expectation that we fulfill our obligation to Him. Here we see the Quran narrate the powerful story of the creation of Adam and Eve.

"And [mention, O Muhammad], when your Lord said to the angels, "Indeed, I will make upon the earth a successive authority." They said, "Will You place upon it one who causes corruption therein and sheds blood, while we declare Your praise and sanctify You?" Allah said, "Indeed, I know that which you do not know."

And He taught Adam the names - all of them. Then He showed them to the angels and said, "Inform Me of the names of these, if you are truthful."

They said, "Exalted are You; we have no knowledge except what You have taught us. Indeed, it is You who is the Knowing, the Wise."

He said, "O Adam, inform them of their names." And when he had informed them of their names, He said, "Did I not tell you that I know the unseen [aspects] of the heavens and the earth? And I know what you reveal and what you have concealed."

And [mention] when We said to the angels, "Prostrate before Adam"; so they prostrated, except for Iblees (satan). He refused and was arrogant and became of the disbelievers."
(Surah Al Baqarah 2:30–34)

In subsequent narrations, when Adam and Eve are tempted by Iblees to eat fruit of the forbidden tree, they realize they had done wrong and repent. Allah accepts their repentance and then places them on Earth, as was His plan (as seen in the very first line of the story above- I will make upon the earth a successive authority). This recognition is crucial to understanding that Adam and Eve were not expelled from Heaven for any sin, but because Allah had planned this for them. This is a significant departure from the Judeo-Christian theology or concepts of "original sin." On the contrary, the one who was expelled from Heaven was Iblees. The cause of his expulsion--arrogance.

In this narration and several others (2:30, 6:165, 10:17) Allah emphasizes the mission He has charged man with: "I have made you a Viceroy on Earth." In contrast to the Judeo-Christian concept of man being cast out as a fallen sinner, the Quran exalts him by saying that man is the best of his creations on Earth (the only one that can communicate by verbal and written word).

During the Prophet's ministry in Mecca, he and his small group faced great opposition. They suffered physical and mental abuse, separation, hunger, and even the threat of death. During this time, the

Prophet learns about the lives of past prophets who faced nearly identical problems. Abraham could not convert his father and Noah could not convert his son. The rich and the privileged were always the most resistant.

Prophet Moses is mentioned most in the Quran (125 times). His story is laid out in great detail, showing his trials and tribulations, his humanity and his shortcomings, his doubts and growth, and the guidance given to him by Allah. We learn that Allah made a covenant with the Jews. He blessed them and made them the chosen people on Earth. But even after all of Moses's miracles, the Jews broke their covenant when Moses left them for forty days. The passages from the Quran reiterate that Allah's blessings come with responsibilities. When people break this covenant, Allah sends down His punishment, both in this world and an even more severe one in the next. He gives the examples of many other prophets including Noah, Lot, Saleh, Hud, Shuaib, David, and Solomon. These stories are meant to remind the Prophet (pbuh) that his situation is no different than his predecessors. Therefore he should not lose heart if people do not listen to him. His role is simply to deliver the message--the Noble Quran. The Quran warns the Prophet that people will call him names, they will tell him he is possessed, that he is a sorcerer, a madman. This is all despite the fact that they knew him well and had already recognized him as the best amongst themselves.

Allah constantly reminds the listener that the message of the Quran is no different from the message delivered by Abraham and all the other prophets who came after him. Each delivered a message in their own language, so that the people who heard it could understand it clearly. As such, the Quran was delivered in Arabic for the people of Arabia. The Quran repeatedly harkens back to the story of Abraham emphasizing his constant centrality to the religion of God and that the Prophet's (pbuh) message (Quran) is nothing other than a continuum of the same message that Abraham delivered to his people.

The second group that the Quran addresses in the Meccan period is the early Believers. This was a small group who accepted Muhammad (pbuh) as the prophet of Allah. They came to believe with no worldly enticement; rather they were moved by a heartfelt recognition of the rightness of the belief in one God, the Creator, the Sustainer, and the Compassionate. The message of the Quran resonated in their hearts as the one and only truth for which they were willing to sacrifice their family, their wealth, and even their lives. During the Meccan period, the believers are taught the essential creed (aqeedah) of a Muslim. In contrast, the Medinan revelations give much more attention to articulating the roles and responsibilities of believers.

The bulk of the Meccan Quran is devoted to the disbelievers. These were the elite of Meccan society and included some of the closest family members of the Prophet (pbuh). The Quran lays out example after example of the blessings that Allah has given to mankind. Any thinking person would realize that everything he possesses is a gift from his Creator. To some He has given much, and to others He has given less. Yet the more He gives, the less thankful man gets. Allah asks the unbelievers to look around them, at the harmony of His creation, how the sun does not overtake the moon, nor the moon overtakes the sun. How the salt water and fresh water come together and yet are separate. How the rainfall brings crops to life and how the Earth brings forth its abundance for us to enjoy. So why worship idols that have no power to do anything? Why reject Allah after witnessing His favors?

Allah relates the stories of the prophets (stories that the Meccans were unaware of), to emphasize how those who reject the truth were punished severely. The Meccans were well aware of the ruined Arab civilizations before them, as they could see the ruins along their caravan routes. Allah relates the story of Moses and his interaction with the Pharaoh of Egypt. Even after seeing the miracle that Moses orchestrated, Pharaoh's arrogance blinded him from the truth and led him to his death. These stories are for the disbelievers to take heed.

When the Meccans challenged Muhammad (pbuh) to bring them a miracle so that they might believe, the Quran told the Prophet that these people are no different from previous generations. Even if they were shown a clear miracle, they still would not believe. The Meccans also took strong exception to the idea of resurrection and final judgment. The Quran explains that those who had followed Allah's directions would be rewarded, while those who had rejected Allah and His prophets would be severely punished. Allah gives a full description of this punishment. It will be a severe fire of molten rocks and there will not be even a drop of water to quench one's thirst. No one will be able to intercede for the disbelievers, and even their hands, feet and tongue will bear witness against them. Hearing all of this, the Meccan's scoffed at the Prophet. They did not believe resurrection was possible. They disputed what they heard and what they already knew, especially the Jews and Christians, who knew from their own books that this was true but still rejected the Prophet's message.

During the Meccan period, Allah also correctly prophesied that some of the Prophet's chief opponents would meet a painful death (Abu Jahl, Abu Lahab and his wife). Finally, after over a decade of unbearable opposition Allah permitted the Prophet to leave Mecca and migrate to the city of Medina.

20 | THE QURAN IN MEDINA

Building an Islamic community.

When the persecution of the Prophet became intolerable in Mecca, Allah gave the Prophet permission to migrate to Yathrib (Medina). The ground for this event had already been prepared by the first and second Aqaba pacts. This migration in 610 C.E. was a singular event with great consequences in the history of Islam. During the subsequent 10 years of the Prophet's life, the last one-third of the Quran was revealed. The gist of these revelations addressed three main audiences. The first is the Prophet (pbuh), the second is the believers, and the third is to the hypocrites.

The Quran now guides the Prophet (pbuh) in establishing and building a true Islamic community. The Muslims are no longer an oppressed minority, but an autonomous community. During this time, the Quran uses the small personal life events and large military challenges and conflicts as living examples to frame Islamic life. At times it even admonishes the Prophet (pbuh) when the Prophet's gentle nature gets in the way of managing statehood, when tough challenges require seemingly harsh decisions.

In addition, the Prophet (pbuh) had to undertake almost twenty-three expeditions during these last ten years of his life. Some were for the protection of the nascent Islamic community in Medina. Some were to neutralize external threats to the community from near and far. During these outings, the Quran brought guidance and assurance to both the Prophet and to the community of believers. In sum, this guidance outlined the totality of a Muslim's commitment to Allah and the Prophet (pbuh). The Quran says, "Allah has purchased from the believers their lives and their properties [in exchange] for that they will have Paradise," (Surah Tauba 9:111). This is the essential covenant between a true believer (Sabiqoon) and his Lord. By living up to this covenant, Allah grants victory after victory to the Prophet (pbuh) and his followers. The Quran describes how Allah helped in these victories when the believers were few and the enemy was powerful and many. These verses assure the Prophet (pbuh) of Allah's promise. It reassures the believers that their mission would indeed be successful so long as they do not follow the path of previous nations like Bani Isra'il who forsook their prophets and abandoned their covenant with Allah.

The Quran also deals with many of the social issues faced by the Prophet (pbuh) and his community in Medina. It grants permission to the Prophet to marry several wives (including his adopted son's divorced wife Zainab) and also deals with his relationship with his adopted child (Zaid ibn Harith). The verses provide guidance on inheritance and the proper division of booty. It also instructs the wives of the Prophet on how to dress, behave, and carry themselves as the "mothers of the believers." Most significantly the Quran establishes the special status that Allah has conferred on the Prophet (pbuh) both among his followers and amongst all of His creation. This unique message in the Quran highlights the unique status conferred upon the Prophet (pbuh). It not only reminds us how Allah regards the Prophet (pbuh), but of our duty to honor him with the highest love and obedience.

"Indeed, Allah showers His blessings upon the Prophet, and His angels pray for him. O believers! Invoke Allah's blessings upon him, and salute him with worthy greetings of peace."
(Surah Ahzab 33: 56)

The Quran also instructs the companions to be mindful of the Prophet's comfort and time. While the people wanted to spend every minute in the Prophet's presence, the Quran instructs them not to abuse his generosity. In fact, it clearly states that they must give him space and time to spend with his family and for rest.

Unlike during the Meccan period, the Medinan Surahs are no longer concerned much with the unbelievers except to tell them that none of their scheming will come to fruition. Rather, much of this portion of the Quran is dedicated to guiding the believers and reminding them of the rewards that await them in Jannah (Heaven). Said another way, the Meccan surahs taught the believers how to drive a car, while the Medinan verses showed them how to drive the car in traffic. The Medinan surahs list these rules and regulations, not to put obstacles in the believer's path but to make his journey safe along the straight road back to Him.

"Those who believe (in Allah) and do righteous deeds – We will surely admit them among the righteous [into Paradise]"
Surah Al Ankabut 29:9)

This straight road is not without its obstacles, dangers, and detours. Many previous nations have incurred the wrath of Allah by going astray and after He had shown His favor to them. Like 'Ad and Thamud, they were wiped off the face of the Earth. For this reason, Allah has set up guard- rails for us (Shariah), so that we can safely stay on the straight path, protecting us from the errors and the failings of past civilizations.

The world that we live in has many attractions and diversions that take us away from the path Allah has defined for us. Therefore, Allah has outlined two key elements to keep us safe. The first is to keep Allah's remembrance foremost in our mind, and this He codified in the nature and frequency of Ibadah (worship). This is how we stay attached to our Creator regardless of what the day brings. After all, Allah says that the prayer is not for Him, it is for us to stay close to Him. The second element that Allah has established for our safety are regulations that deal with social issues of interpersonal relationships (marriage, divorce, inheritance, family responsibilities, business transactions, dietary issues, etc.). All of these guidelines are exemplified in the excellence and personality of the Prophet (pbuh). Sincerity, humility, honesty, trust, gratitude, patience, and perseverance are some of the essentials in achieving success. These traits help us avoid the pitfalls and potholes we encounter along our journey.

Perhaps the biggest obstacle to our ultimate success is the single trait that takes us away from Allah: arrogance. Arrogance was what expelled Iblees from Paradise. Arrogance also pulled the Pharaoh to the bottom of the sea. Man foolishly thinks he knows shortcuts to Paradise. He often thinks he knows the way, better than what Allah has made known to him. He is fooling no one but himself, and Allah asks us to beware of following such examples. At the same time Allah asks us to beware of excessive zeal in pseudo-religiosity. In one sentence Allah summarizes the essence of Muslim identity:

> *"It is not righteousness that you turn your faces towards the East and the West, but righteous is the one who believes in Allah, and the Last Day, and the angels and the Book and the prophets, and gives away wealth out of love for Him to the near of kin and the orphans and the needy and the wayfarer and to those who ask and to set slaves free and keeps up prayer and pays the poor-rate; and the performers of their promise when they make a promise, and the patient in distress and affliction and in the time of conflict. These are they who are truthful; and these are they who keep their duty."*
> *(Surah Al Baqarah. 2:177)*

The core message of Islamic practice is to care for those who are less fortunate than you. In fact, the injunction for giving charity is mentioned fifty-nine times in the Quran, considerably more than even the establishment of prayer. The difference between charity and prayer is that Allah loves your acts of charity, whereas prayer is only a means for you to remember Allah and stay close to him.

"Those who (in charity) spend of their goods by night and by day, in secret and in public, have their reward with their lord: on them shall be no fear, nor shall they grieve." (Surah Al Baqarah 2:274)

The Quran also provides a multitude of supplications (duas) that are most pleasing to Allah. These dua remind us that we are truly helpless and depend solely on Allah's mercy. These supplications also are designed to teach us gratitude, patience and perseverance.

The third category of people that are addressed in the Medinan verses are the hypocrites. These are the people who came into Islam for the socio-economic benefits rather than personal convictions. They might loudly proclaim their love for the Prophet (pbuh), but when called to join in military expeditions, they were the first to withdraw with flimsy excuses. The Quran warns the Prophet (pbuh) to be wary of such people who will ultimately suffer the most severe punishment:

"Allah has promised the hypocrite men and the hypocrite women and the infidels, the Fire of Hell, to abide in it forever. That is enough for them, Allah has cursed them, and for them is a lasting chastisement." (Surah At Tauba 9:68)

This is a clear warning to all those who divide their loyalties between Allah and their own desires and are fooling no one but themselves. The Medinan verses explain that while ignorance is one thing, hypocrisy is much worse. Many millennia ago, Abraham prayed to Allah on the plains of Arafat:

"My Lord, make this city secure and distance me and my children from worshipping the idols." (Surah Al Baqarah 2:126)

Allah answered that prayer by sending us the Prophet who returned us to the religion of Abraham (millat Ibrahim). In dramatic fashion, Allah sent one of the final verses of the Quran where Abraham made his dua:

"This day I have perfected your religion, completed my favor upon you, and have chosen for you Islam as your religion."
(Surah Al Maida 5:3).

With this verse, Allah completed the circle that began with Abraham and culminated with the Prophet Muhammed (pbuh):

"Say, [O believers], 'We have believed in Allah and what has been revealed to us and what has been revealed to Abraham and Ishmael and Isaac and Jacob and the Descendants and what was given to Moses and Jesus and what was given to the prophets from their Lord. We make no distinction between any of them, and we are Muslims [in submission] to Him.'" (Surah Al Baqarah 2:136)

21 | THE DISEASED HEART

Dishonesty and deceit is a Muslim's greatest enemy.

New York, London, Madrid, Boston, and now Paris--the terror marches on and on. Repeatedly young Muslim men have taken it upon themselves to fight the world in a warped sense of justice. Blowing up buildings, taking innocent lives, and creating general mayhem have become their way of protest, all in the name of Islam. It is sad to watch events unfold again and again but what is sadder still is to watch the stream of platitudes from Muslim leaders that fill our TV and radio waves after each of these horrific events. The pattern is always the same after each successive act of wanton terrorism. Every one of these "leaders" wants to distance himself from the perpetrators. They are labeled extremists. They are brainwashed. They are not acting in the spirit of Islam. Islam means "peace" and Islam is a peaceful religion. I am sure they believe that their efforts create a buffer between the "bad" Muslims and the "good" Muslims.

Over and over we hear the Quranic ayah being quoted that, "the taking of one life is as if you had killed the whole of mankind," (Quran 5:32). Unfortunately, no one believes these statements anymore.

Remember the old adage "fool me once–shame on you, fool me twice –shame on me."   People of the world are not fools to be taken in with words again and again. As much as we would not like to admit it, they see that there is something fundamentally wrong with many Muslims today. In fact, they see Islam as a violent religion and as long as we continue to cast a veil over our shortcomings, we are destined to see these horrible events repeat themselves in other cities. The only way out of this spiral is to face up to the fact that "yes" there is something wrong with the way Muslims "practice" Islam today that breeds the type of individuals that feel no compunction in killing innocent men, women, and children. Unless we engage in an honest self-analysis, we cannot get to the root cause of the cancer in our community and find real solutions to our problems.

What has become of Islam today? What are we missing? Look at the Muslim world. While there are people of sincerity and honesty, there is also widespread injustice. Most Muslims live in an environment of physical, cultural, economic, and/or sectarian oppression. This seems to be most prevalent in Muslim-majority countries. Those in power are constantly expanding their share of the world. Those at the margins see that their only options lie in a violent grab for their share.

In addition to widespread oppression, a new phenomenon has emerged in recent times: the individual has become the center of his universe, at the expense of the community. This is a Western concept. But whereas the West had developed institutions that tried to balance the rights of the community against the rights of the individual, the Muslim world, which has recently emerged from colonial rule has not developed similar institutions that protect the community. Therefore the individual free-for-all we see in many Muslim-majority countries has become the norm. Corruption, deceit, and dishonesty have become routine at all levels of society. Is this Islam? What are we missing?

Islam was never a religion of the individual, by the individual, for the individual. When Islam was a dominant civilization it was always a community-based religion. The well-being of the community was paramount, not the well-being of a single individual. The social norms of behavior enjoined on Muslims were always to protect the welfare of the community often at the expense of the individual even in some of the simple aspects of life such as prohibitions on usury (interest) and drunkenness. The life of the Prophet (pbuh) was a constant struggle to build a community and make them successful.

It is also critical to point out that Islam was never a peaceful religion nor was it a violent religion. Islam was always a religion of struggle. There was always a constant struggle both within the hearts and minds of the Muslims and the civilization they lived in. The pre-Islamic Jahili Meccans started to develop a philosophy of individual elitism. The Prophet struggled to undo this trend. The community of mutual helpers in Medina not only included the Muslims but also their non-Muslim neighbors. In Islam the struggle is not on behalf of oneself but a fight against oppression and injustice that the whole community experiences and especially for the welfare of the weak, poor, and disenfranchised. By promoting Islam as a religion of peace we have disempowered Muslims from the great good that they can do in this world. Islam has become a passive religion where the pursuit of individual goals is built around ritual worship. "Peace" has become a substitute for non-engagement. Success is defined by personal wealth, and religion is just a superficial veneer of false-virtue. When the pursuit of wealth is shut off for people at the margins of society, the warped messages from the pulpit become siren calls for deliverance from injustice. Religion is jettisoned for irrational behavior and the result plays out in massacre after massacre.

Where is the alternate narrative of Islam? The alternate narratives all seem to be in the past. The historic glories of the Islamic civilization seem so far out of our reach. There are few Muslim organizations fighting against oppression and injustice today. Did not God appoint us Muslims as his "viceroy" on Earth? (khalifa). Where are the Muslim organizations trying to care for the environment, protecting the land and the seas, saving the many species that are going extinct, or even making life better for humans by their discoveries and contributions? Where are the great centers of learning that attract the best and the brightest? There are over sixty International NGO organizations fighting to protect the Earth's fauna and flora. Not one of these has Muslim leadership or significant Muslim participation. Why have we left it to the non-Muslims to do all the heavy lifting? Why is there an International Criminal Court and not a Muslim Court of justice that can hold oppressors culpable for the wrongs they do? More Muslims are killed at the hands of other Muslims than non-Muslims, all in the name of religion. So whose religion and what religion are we talking about? When the Organization of Islamic States (OIC) and other organizations meet every year, do they have any relevance to the life of ordinary Muslims or are they just a reunion of well-to-do leaders?

A Muslim Court of Justice built to the highest ideals of Islam can provide Muslims with a direction for engagement and action to fight injustices, exploitation, and oppression. Western countries have developed a process of economic ostracization (sanctions) against human right violations. The community of Muslims if galvanized through the direction of a Muslim Court of Justice could use a similar approach to marginalize the oppressors and oppressing countries. They would have a larger impact due to their sheer size than even the International Criminal Court. No magazine would dare deface the Prophet (pbuh) if the Muslim court were to place sanctions against all French products and services. And when ordinary Muslims see that they are an integral part of redressing injustice they would no longer need to resort to extremist behavior. Absent this effort, Muslims on the street feel rudderless, disconnected, and easy prey to hucksters who recruit them as tools for personal agendas and violence. Is it any wonder, that the weaker minds among us feel no pride in the capacity religion can be used for good, but instead fall prey to the message of conspiracies and victimhood blared repeatedly from the pulpit? All they have to aspire to is the constant race for material gain they see around them. Even they can see that this was never the purpose of their religion.

Let us then admit that we are failing our community as much as the terrorists are. We are the victims of our own self-centered material pursuits and have shirked our moral responsibilities.

Where is the solution? Many have turned to the mosques for answers. In fact, mosques today are increasingly packed with worshippers. Unfortunately, more prayers, more fasting, and more Umrah and Hajj do not appear to be providing the answers. Instead this seems to be making us even less tolerant of the rest of the world. Additionally, passive piety has taken the place of action. The Quran warns us that, "Allah will not change the condition of a people unless they change themselves" (13: 11). So waiting for God cannot be the answer. Rather God is waiting for us.

In its heyday, Islam was a communal religion and there was no force that could stop its dominance. Before we can even think of changing the world (too large an abstract idea) we need to focus our attention inwardly. What does it mean to be a Muslim? Is the "shahadah" enough? Is praying five times a day enough?

The Prophet Muhammad (peace be upon him) was asked, "Can a believer be a coward?" The Prophet said, "Yes." He was then asked, "Can a believer be a miser?" He replied, "Yes." And finally, he was asked, "Can a believer be a liar?" The Prophet said: "No." (Al Muwatta, Vol 56, 19)

This points to the crux of our problem. We lie to each other as a matter of convenience. We lie to ourselves to justify our selfish behaviors in our headlong pursuit of worldly gain. We lie to Allah when we promise to be better, but never make the effort. Is it any wonder the rampant corruption, deceit and arrogance that have become the hallmark of our civilization today? Our societies are built on the pillars of overt and hidden deceit. We have perfected the art of lying because we practice it daily, but make excuses that it preserves respectability. Should God listen to the prayers of the dishonest? Why should God respond to our tearful pleas if our hearts are turned away in disobedience?

When wealth is the measure of success in society as it is today, people lie because their self-interest comes before the wellbeing of others and in that process, their cheating and deceit destroys community after community. Graft and corruption that have overtaken the Muslim world are the result of one failing - dishonesty. There is a self-delusion that we can still be Muslim while lying our way to riches and power. Looking to the government to solve the problems of corruption is part of the self-delusion because the government only reflects the prevailing attitudes of the people that elect it. No! The message has to be drilled into every Muslim in the home and the mosque: "You are not a Muslim if you are not truthful." It is not important how many times you bow your head in prayer. It is no use to pretend otherwise. You will be cut off from God's mercy and help. At every moment in time, a Muslim must ask the question of himself, "Have I lied today?" Then ask, "Have I done any good today?" and lastly ask, "Have I hurt someone today?" If the answers are "no, yes, no," then only can he truly call himself an earnest Muslim. And the dua of an earnest Muslim will never go unanswered.

The companions of the Prophet (pbuh) met these criteria, which is why they left behind an example of unparalleled success. This community distinguished themselves by what they gave rather than what they received. Collectively they fought against injustice, arrogance, and tyranny. Collectively they overcame obstacles that they would not have been able to as individuals.

As individuals in Mecca, the Muslims were open to discrimination, vilification and disenfranchisement. In contrast, when they were in Medina they were able to withstand and prosper against overwhelming odds to establish a vibrant civilization. We need to learn from this example so that we can shed our victim mentality and adopt something far more positive. People gravitate towards success and if the examples of success are the number of people you can kill, the results will be accordingly. On the other hand, if Muslims are seen as the leaders making their communities better places, even the weak-minded will gravitate toward the latter.

To say a Muslim should be scrupulously honest, of course is easier said than done. After all, honesty and integrity are rare to find these days. The first one to be exploited and taken advantage of is the honest man. The only redress is to be part of a constituency of honest men where you are no longer an isolated individual that can be steamrolled by the dishonest. This is precisely why Islam is a communal religion and can be practiced only within a community of honest people, and not as an individual. Muslims are failing not because their worship is weak but their communities no longer exit.

How can we establish Muslim communities? Firstly, we need to define what we mean by community. A community is not just the Muslims surrounding us. A community is the place we live in, work in, and play in. A community includes all our neighbors, Muslim and non-Muslim. The presence of a Muslim in any group of people should be felt as a breath from Paradise. A Muslim should be the first person people turn to, to find help with their difficulties. This is because everything they do is based on honesty and integrity.

The Quran says again and again, "believe in Allah and do good deeds..." But deeds can only be good if they are performed with integrity. An act of kindness goes a long way to making the community better. A smile is a great introduction to your inner self and costs nothing. Making eye contact with your neighbors and being respectful of their space begins a process of engagement. Inviting people into your home, exchanging cards and gifts on "their" holidays is an expression that you value them as neighbors. Stepping into community activities, lending your support and ideas, and volunteering, all go a long way to strengthening your community. Just imagine what would happen if even a fraction of the two billion Muslims that populate the world were to engage in this process! It would bring about a revolution in the well-being of mankind that would be unprecedented. But remember, it is a fight that cannot happen at the individual level, it is a fight that can only be won at a communal level.

22 | THE WEST VERSUS ISLAM

Arrogance has prevented the West from understanding Islam.

A friend recently asked me, "Why do Americans and Europeans have so much difficulty understanding Islam?" The question got me thinking about a recent theory put forward by some geneticists (Dean Hamer), who have proposed that human DNA contains a "GOD GENE." According to this hypothesis, the human brain is hardwired to believe in spiritual experiences that can be measured by psychometric methods, and these tendencies are partially heritable (Wikipedia). Archaeologists Joyce Marcus and Kent Flannery have studied religion in the temples of the Oaxaca Valley of Mexico. They argue that religion is an evolved behavior favored by natural selection. Its universal presence in all societies suggests that it is "wired into our neural circuitry before the ancestral human population dispersed from its African homeland." (NYTimes Nov 14 2009). According to these scientists, the two conditions that control spirituality seem to be our genes and our evolutionary background. The fine balance between these two elements determines what a person is willing to believe and accept, or disbelieve and reject.

The Islamic concept of spirituality rejects that genetics has anything to do with spirituality. Instead Muslims believe that every human being is created with a soul that reflects the Creator. This soul is the "ruh" which resides in the heart and is as a lamp which shines bright when the spiritual connection to his Creator is high and dims as the connection decreases or is faint and extinguished in some. Whether it is the "ruh" or the god-gene, there exists in all humans an intrinsic and inherent spirituality that they are born with.

The harsh climate conditions of primitive hunter-gatherer societies that migrated out of Africa to the northern cold lands of Europe fostered an environment of survival-of-the-fittest as a necessary part of human evolution. Hunter-gatherers soon developed skills and technology to master their environment. Social evolution led to congregated societies that often required a unifying theme to maintain social order. Religion was the answer built around a supernatural phenomena often in the form of nature such as thunder, lightning, rain, Sun, Moon, etc. As the proficiency of their skills increased, they became hunter-conquerors by subjugating other humans often in the name of their new theology. The more successful they were in these endeavors, the more their "self-belief" in their physical and intellectual prowess diminished the need for a reliance on a transcendental Creator/God for their success. "Self worship" soon replaced "self-belief." The balance between spirituality and the social evolution tilted heavily towards the latter. Any credit to the supernatural became inconvenient to maintain power amongst the elites. However, spirituality could not be totally suppressed among the masses, and so it was easier to co-opt their spiritual instincts by overlaying human attributes of power over belief in a supernatural being creating "pseudo-socio-religions." A good example is the concept of the Holy Roman Emperor anointed by Popes as specially chosen by God and/or transcended from God as with the Caesars of Rome who were considered "sons" of God." It became important that each successful tribe/civilization create its unique religious identity to distinguish its elite religious and social status.

This phenomenon is not unique to Western civilization. It also infects some Islamic societies. The phenomenon is directly correlated with the desire to establish physical, cultural, social and economic dominance over other humans. The spiritual need to "believe" then becomes a tool to be used and manipulated to achieve this aim. Any idea that challenges the skewed balance between power and spirituality is therefore rejected. Every prophet was opposed and resisted by the elite. What the Pharaoh did to Moses (pbuh), what the Pharisees did to Jesus (pbuh), and what the Meccans did to Muhammed (pbuh) are clear examples of the corruption of religion when it is controlled by the state. In Jesus's famous sermon on the mount, he said, "Blessed [are] the meek: for they shall inherit the earth" (Mathew 5:5). This clearly indicates that aristocracy and true spirituality are incompatible.

When you strip the rituals and dogma from religion, the core of spirituality is quite simple. In Islam, it is "Believe in a Creator and do good in this world." The prophets understood this message. The sages understood this message. But the elites always struggled with it. It is none other than the "Golden Rule" that every religion teaches. Jesus said, "Do unto others as you would have them do unto you" (Matthew 7:12). Buddhist documents from the 6th century BCE include the quote, "Hurt not others in ways that you yourself would find hurtful." Earlier texts from the Mahabharata read, "Do not unto others which would cause pain if done to you" (5:15:17). Hillel, the famous Jewish rabbi said, "That which is hateful to you, do not do to your fellow. That is the whole Torah; the rest is the explanation; go and learn." Islam goes further where the Prophet said, "None of you truly believes until he wishes for his brother that which he wishes for himself." Thus it is not only doing good or harm that is important but even your thoughts that define your spirituality.

There are in religion a whole list of obligatory commands and admonishments that are often translated into ritual maxims. Over time these rituals obscure the spirit of religion, and form replaces substance. "How" you worship becomes more important than "why" you worship. Piety is expressed more to be seen by others than to be seen by God, and heads are bowed more by the weight of riches than by the humility of the heart. The Quran says:

Have you seen him who denies the Final Judgment?

Then such is the man who repulses the orphan (with harshness), and encourages not the feeding of the indigent.

So woe to those praying ones, Who are careless of their prayers,

Those who (want but) to be seen (of men), but refuse (to supply) (even) small neighborly needs." (Surah Al Ma'un 107:1–7)

In most evolving societies, religion became a tool of the state to control the masses. At the beginning this may have conferred compelling advantages in promoting unity of ideals and purposeful behavior. However, as communities became larger, more and more rituals were introduced not to emphasize theology but to protect the power of the elite. The result of this process is that as power became more centralized, greater degrees of arrogance and delusion became part of religion. Pseudo-spirituality became the source of power, and power became the source of spirituality. This is the reason why so many kings of yesteryear claimed direct descent from deities and fought political wars in the name of religion. Over time, the line between what was real and what was socio-evolutionary acceptance to deify power became blurred. The concept of the Creator/God was muted at the expense of amplified human attributes. The fundamental change was the re-creation of God from his infinite and transcendent nature to that of a super human being. This is the arrogance of man. It is no longer the words of God through His prophets that define Him but man chooses to define God within his own intellect. The laws of God no longer apply to him, and the technological advances especially of the modern age, give him the freedom to choose his own path where God is no longer deemed necessary or important. This has become the dominant theology of the West.

God is depicted in the famous painting of Michael Angelo and others as a Santa Claus like figure. He makes mistakes in creation and has to redeem Himself. This is classic humanizing of the transcendental Creator. This is arrogance that borders on "shirk." This change has occurred unrestrained over many millennia in the Northern Hemisphere such that the European psyche only believes in "power-theologies" because they consciously or not promote "self worship." In most other parts of the world, this process has repeatedly been interrupted by a succession of prophets and saints that have reset the balance between spirituality and the evolutionary impulses for "self worship." That is why religions that have migrated to Europe have been corrupted by the inclusion of human theology that is in contradiction to the messages of the prophets that the human self is the instrument of the Creator and not the other way around. Christianity, the dominant religion of the West, rejected the essential teaching of Jesus in the importance of maintain the God-given Laws of the Torah. Instead Christianity adopted the Pauline theology that overrode and abrogated God's laws. God's law no longer applied to man.

Islam, in its purest form, personalized religion between the Creator and the individual and removed all human attributes to God. Man was created to serve God as his only Master, and the rich and the powerful had no dominion over the believer or could change any of God's laws. His was an unseen God revealed through the prophets who tasked man to go out and do good in this world. Power was only a tool to promote justice in this world. Prophet Mohammed (pbuh) said during his last sermon, "You are equal. Nobody has superiority over others, except by piety and good actions." The absence of a human power elite or humanized intercessor between God and man contradicts the evolutionary mindset of the European races where "self worship" and a theology determined by humans is not only accepted but expected. The result, therefore, is that the people of the Western hemisphere have subordinated their "ruh" or god-gene to the extent that they are now culturally programmed against understanding the true, unfiltered, unmediated relationship with the Creator. This mutated suppression of the "ruh"/ god-gene is the fundamental reason why they are incapable of understanding Islam. As the Quran says:

"Allah hath set a seal on their hearts and on their hearing, and on their eyes is a veil." (Surah Al Baqarah 2:7)

Islamic theology tells us that the elites are not masters, but servants charged with the welfare of the community. That the European race remained blind to Islam is therefore a gift from Allah, for it was not co-opted by the Europeans at their time of maximum global ascendancy (18-20th centuries). This was a time when learning was restricted to the elite and at a time when Islam could easily have been corrupted like previous prophetic traditions. In the 21st century, Islam therefore retains the purity of its beliefs free of human machinations and free of a socio-religious aristocracy. The peripheral influence of the West may have dimmed the true spirit of Islam in the collective consciousness of the community of Muslims, but the religion remains largely uncorrupted. A personal connection between a believer and his Creator remains the same as it did 1400 years ago.

Yet the obvious and important reason why people in the West hate Islam is because of their willful ignorance and deliberate desire to avoid learning about it. It challenges their sense of superiority even when it comes to an understanding of God. As such, true Islam is the last line of defense holding back the world from hurtling headlong into a Godless, hedonistic world of instant gratification and selfish desires.

23 | A REVIVAL PLAN

Commual living and sharing is the only path to Islamic revival.

When I look at Muslims in the world today, I see a weak echo of the great Islamic civilizations of the past. As a scientist, I find that Muslims have lost sight of a key focus of what made previous civilizations so great. Muslims have lost a sense of community and purpose. Without these, we are unlikely to change our overall condition. Muslims have bought wholly into the Western ideology of individualism and self-gratification.

So when we talk of revitalization of Islam, we really mean the revitalization of the community. Though many of us may be very successful professionals and practicing Muslims, our lifestyle remains incomplete. When we talk of returning to the fundamentals of Islam, it is not the intensity and quantity of prayer and fasting, but the uplifting of community. But if we hope to achieve this enterprising goal, we need to develop an organized strategy that all community members can buy into.

Narrative:

The Muslim nation is in crisis. In spite of almost a third of the world's population and a third of Muslim majority countries in the world, Muslim populations are under siege worldwide. Yet there are more Muslims who perform religious obligations of Salat and Sawm, more Muslims at Umra and Hajj every year, more prayers sent up to heaven for deliverance from the dominance from non-Muslim populations with very few apparent results. In this helpless state, generations of Muslim youth are getting disconnected from their Islamic roots because they see a disconnect between all the piety of religion and the reality of personal existence. Why is there this disconnect? Scholars repeatedly expound the thesis that we are disconnected from our Islamic roots and therefore are in this miserable state of disorder, helpless and disunited. However, in spite of thousands of books, lectures, discourses, and exhortations, we lack a singular action plan that could take the "Ummah" back to its roots.

What are these roots and how do we get back to it? In my humble opinion it is not the focus on ever more ritual performances or recitation. Rather we need to embrace the communal approach that Islam teaches us. The West champions individualism, because for a long time it was locked in a Dark Age of feudalism that purposefully kept most people illiterate. Those who could break these shackles eventually helped bring Europe out of its despair. However, Muslims were never subject to these conditions. Knowledge was not only freely accessible, it was required. Slavery and servitude were considered undesirable. Muslims thrived on the concept of being one community where the welfare of each individual was the collective responsibility of the whole. Allah also made this very clear in the Quran:

"Let there be a community among you, advocating what is good, demanding what is right, and eradicating what is wrong; these are indeed the successful." (Surah Al Imran 3:104)

In his book on Islam, Professor William Cantwell Smith, summarized that, "The building of a proper community life is a supreme imperative" of the Islamic endeavor.

It is not that the Muslim ulema do not recognize the full importance of creating a community. In fact, they often publicly plead with Allah to unite the hearts of Muslims. But without a clear strategy, this is nothing but whistling in the dark. It is as if we are all on a kindergarten soccer team chasing around a shiny new ball without knowing the true purpose of the game, nor how to even score a goal. Rather we are merely told to run harder and kick harder, hoping that that alone will earn us a trophy. If we get tired, God will give us the points we need.

What is it that our scholars are unable to communicate to the greater community? Our failure to find real world answers might be due to our proclivity to over-intellectualize the Islamic sciences. Perhaps scholars are drowning the average Muslim mind with an avalanche of information as a way to sustain their leadership in society. In the process, we are all losing the "forest for the trees."

The real key to success of the Islamic civilization was self-sacrifice for the larger good of the community. You have to ask yourself, why did the Prophet (pbuh) go around with stones tied to his middle to stave off hunger? Did he, the political leader of the community, not have enough resources to buy food? After all, was he not entitled to one-fifth of all the booty the Muslims won in the battles against Qureysh and other Arab tribes? He should have been the wealthiest man in Arabia. Yet he often had nothing to eat and occasionally survived on a few dates that people brought to him. The answer is quite simple. He gave everything he had for the welfare of the community. This was the Prophet's (pbuh) secret to success. He taught us that collective engagement is far better than individual effort. "One for all and all for one," is not just a motto from The Three Musketeers, but the secret of all successful civilizations and empires.

When we talk about reclaiming our heritage, we have to start at the beginning. How do we recreate the Muslim community, in an age when we have become so separated from one another?

I believe there always has been an answer. If we look at the companions of the Prophet (pbuh), few of them knew the entire Quran (much of it had not yet been revealed fully until much later), yet many of them were the best of Muslims. What was the secret that the Prophet (pbuh) used to transform a uneducated society into the best ummah imaginable? I believe it was the clarity and simplicity of his Vision and Mission. Every successful endeavor requires a plan of action. Whether we are building a new business or starting a social movement, we need to begin with a clear vision and defined mission statement. The Prophet (pbuh) understood what Islam called for and how to achieve it.

PLAN FOR ISLAMIC REVIVAL

Vision Statement:

"To regain the Muslim heritage of the great Islamic Civilization."

Mission Statement:

"To establish vibrant successful Muslim Communities that can transform the socio-political, cultural, and religious exceptionalism of Muslims."

Values Statement:

"To be the best human being possible in the service of Allah."

This vision statement distills the essence of what it means to be a Muslim. Allah has appointed us as His viceroy on Earth (2:30) and tasked us to represent Him as embodied in His ninety-nine attributes. Our challenge is to represent Him to the best of our human abilities in embodying these attributes. Therefore, to be the best possible human being in the service of Allah, we have to strive for excellence in our love for Allah and the Prophet (pbuh). We have to strive for excellence in knowledge of the Quran and Sunnah. We have to strive for excellence in our worship and our relationships with our family. We have to strive for excellence in acquiring worldly knowledge and using it to support our communities. We have to strive for excellence in our professions, so that we can best serve our fellow men and also protect the world around us. Only then can we say that we are fulfilling our responsibilities according to the will of Allah and claim to be "the best community raised up for mankind." (Surah Al Imran 3:110)

Imagine the impact on young minds if they grow up with the mindset that they are required to be the best in each and every one of these endeavors. Imagine the impact of telling a non-Muslim about a Muslim's vision of excellence. How would that compare to the typical explanation of what it means to be Muslim, which often leads the questioner more confused than ever before. If every Muslim child grew up with this understanding clearly imprinted on their minds, there would be no limit to what we could achieve. As we can see from the achievements of early Islamic civilizations, Allah has promised to help us with incredible success.

PLAN OF ACTION

Any plan facing the challenge of forming a Muslim community in the modern world is daunting and cannot be accomplished by only holding onto traditional solutions. It must to be a bold multi-pronged approach that is willing to challenge previous methodologies.

The basic plan requires every member of the community to contribute to a central fund that is managed by the structural hierarchy of the community for the prioritized welfare of all members. Unfortunately, the Sunni Muslim community has no centralized authority, which makes this enterprise more challenging. Therefore, I suggest that we begin as a smaller segment of the larger community who is interested in banding together resources to achieve a shared vision. As word grows, more members will be attracted to the cause and can join the founding group. This proposal can be several phases and can start small and as confidence builds up can be taken to its highest level.

PHASE 1| Love of the Prophet (pbuh)

The very first prerequisite for any revival of Islam is for Muslims to fall in love with the Prophet (pbuh). This does not mean just singing songs of praise, but really getting to know the in's and out's of how he lived, his personality, and his interactions with people around him. In other words we have to walk in the shoes of the companions of the Prophet (pbuh) and behave as they did. We have to adopt their sense of commitment and dedication to personal transformation. We must share their sense of sacrifice and their sense of brotherhood. Only this will bring real change and take us from our own jahilyah to becoming men of the Quran—those who Allah is most pleased with. Without this kind of transformation, there is little chance of reviving Islam. One cannot move to Phase 2,3,4 or 5 without an absolute commitment to Phase 1.

PHASE 2| Sharing- Building Trust

In Phase 2, members must commit to making a contribution ranging from 2% to 10% of their monthly income (based on a graduated scale) to a central "Community fund."

Option 1: The collected amount is redistributed equally to all members.

PRO: Members at the lower financial end will benefit and have a more secure position in the community. At the same time, they will be rooting for the more financially successful members to do well, as it will positively impact their own well-being. At the same time, those at the higher end of the financial ladder will be pulling for those below them to do well so that they would get to retain a larger part of the distribution. All members of the community will be helping each other, working and praying for each other's success

CON: Will members try to game the system by not being honest and trustworthy? Given the current environment, this is highly likely. Without full trust in each other, there is no Ummah. It therefore can only include people who believe honesty is fundamental to their Muslim identity. Inshallah, their success will attract others.

Option 2: Only 50% of the community fund is shared as above and the other 50% is utilized for community infrastructure (Masjid, school, refugees, etc. based on community projects).

Option 3: 100% of the Fund is reserved for the community projects, but this option takes away the concept of shared wellness.

PHASE 3| Charitable Giving

At the present time many members give their Zakat and Sadaqah for various local and international charities. It is far more important to give to local charities than the latter. It is the welfare you can affect in and around your neighborhoods that can highlight the true nature of Islam as a religion that demands us to make the world a better place to live in. Giving charity through a pooled resource (i.e. An "Islamic United Way") will have a far more positive impact than the same amount we give as individuals. This would be the same whether it is for humanitarian assistance (soup kitchen, etc.), animal rescue, wildlife preservation, or any other cause.

PHASE 4| Investment

It is important for the community to invest in itself by developing business enterprises that employ community members and also create revenue that can be cycled back into the community. Many talented individuals are hindered by a lack of capital to become successful entrepreneurs. This is where the community can come in and invest in our local talents. Members can benefit from discounted services as well as honest reliable outcomes.

The community can negotiate group rates with a varitey of vendors for better pricing on insurance, travel, purchasing, etc.

PHASE 5| Socio-Political

Having developed a critical mass, the local community can visibly engage in larger, municipal, nation, and global initiatives that require our attention. This could take the form of fighting for the environment, racial equality, human rights, and more. We could also collectively engage in the political process as a voting bloc, which is far more effective than voting as individuals.

Summary

In our current Muslim cultural environment, it is difficult to imagine this strategy succeeding. However, we must remember that most every successful initiative begins as an outside idea championed by just a core group of committed individuals. This was true of the Prophet's (pbuh) mission just as it is true for industry leaders like Facebook, Amazon, and Apple.

24 | CONCLUSION

At the end of the day, the reality of our condition is very simple. We lack honesty. Dishonesty, deceit, racism, zulm, and trampling on the rights of others have become steps on the ladders of success these days. We are not honest with ourselves when we deviate from the path Allah has laid out for us in the Quran and in the example of the Prophet (pbuh). We make excuses, compromises, and put our self-interests before the rights of others. On the contrary, we ought to realistically assess our place in Allah's grand creation. This should humble us and remind us that we were put on Earth to serve Allah by serving his creation. This all goes back to my favorite ayah of the Quran where Allah has made this abundantly clear:

"Righteousness is not that you turn your faces toward the east or the west, but [true] righteousness is [in] one who believes in God, the Last Day, the angels, the Book, and the prophets and gives wealth, in spite of love for it, to relatives, orphans, the needy, the traveler, those who ask [for help], and for freeing slaves; [and who] establishes prayer and gives zakah (obligatory charity); [those who]

fulfill their promise when they promise; and [those who] are patient in poverty and ailment and during battle. Those are the ones who have been true, and it is those who are the righteous."
(Sura Al Baqarah, 2:177)

May Allah give us the strength to live up to His expectations and forgive us our shortcomings! Ameen!

EPILOGUE

My personal journey with the Quran started at a very young age, when my parents hired a Quran tutor to teach me how to read. However, as much as I tried, and as much as my teachers tried (I had not one but several tutors in succession), I had a great difficulty in connecting the Arabic letters and sounding out their attached vowels. In retrospect, I can only surmise that this may have been due to an undiagnosed case of dyslexia that plagued me in every other language I tried to learn. While I struggled with languages, I was always a whiz in mathematics.

All of my siblings finished their first complete reading of the Quran before the age of ten. But I was so far behind that a special uncle, who had come to stay with us in Bombay, took pity on my sorry state and decided that he would read individual words of the Quran slowly so that I could repeat after him. That was how I finished my first completion of the Quran by the age of thirteen. Ever since that first completion, the Quran only came into my hand when someone passed away on the occasion of a khatam-e-Quran. I struggled to read a single juz, and the embarrassing ordeal often lasted well over an hour and a half.

In college, I reapplied myself to Arabic with little improvement. After getting married I would try and read the Quran, but my wife would comment that it sounded like I was spelling out the words. In the end, my solution was to concentrate on a few surahs—namely YaSin and Ar-Rehman—and simply read these over and over again.

Over the years I saw minimal improvement in my fluency. But then seven years ago, something remarkable happened. I was sitting against a pillar in Masjid-e-Nabawi during Ramadan, waiting for the muezzin to make the call for Zuhr prayer. As I was reading the Quran I couldn't help but overhear the gentleman next to me who was reading the Quran with remarkable speed and fluency. I couldn't help but think, "If Allah could just make it easier for me to read the Quran, I would read it so much more!"

A month or two later it dawned on me that my fluency with the Quran had markedly improved. For the first time, I was actually enjoying reading the Quran rather than looking at it as a chore! Recognizing this as Allah's great mercy on me, I have devoted myself to the Quran, and not a day goes by that I have not read some portion of it. It is such a remarkable change in my life that I cannot imagine an outsider being able to appreciate how transformative this experience has been in my life. Since making the Quran a daily habit, my days are less stressful. The recitation of the Quran brings meaning and happiness to my life. The Quran has imbued me with a far greater sense of gratitude to Allah for every single mercy He has showered upon me.

I was often told to read the Quran quietly. I can only imagine this was because I read it so poorly! But the more I read the Quran, the more I came to realize that I am not reading a random book. Rather I am repeating Allah's words. So why should Allah's words be hidden? Ever since I have read the Quran aloud. Beginning each day reciting Allah's spoken word builds a powerful connection between me and my Creator. This connection influences the rest of my day. As I have reached the latter years of my life, I have come to appreciate the Quran very differently. No, it is not just a book to be read. Rather when I read the Quran, Allah is talking to me. What a great blessing for all who recognize this marvelous gift!

ABOUT THE AUTHOR

Mohammed Mohiuddin was born in Hyderabad, India in 1945. He graduated from Osmania Medical College and trained in Oncology at the Royal Marsden Hospital in London. He later immigrated to the United States in 1975 and began a notable career as a physician-scientist. Throughout his career, he has held several prominent positions such as Chairman of Radiation Medicine at the University of Kentucky, and Director of the Cancer Center at Geisinger Health System followed by a six-year directorship at the King Faisal Specialist Hospital in Riyadh, Saudi Arabia. Having authored over 300 scientific articles during his prolific career, he is globally recognized as one of the leading cancer physicians in the United States.

Dr. Mohiuddin is the father of three children who have also pursued careers in medicine. He has retired from medicine and enjoys studying Islam, comparative religion, and playing with his seven grandchildren.